MASTER
FLOWER
FINDER

About the Nature Study Guild . . .

The founder of the Nature Study Guild of Berkeley, California, in 1938, **May Theilgaard Watts** received her training in botany at the University of Chicago and served as staff naturalist and education director at the Morton Arboretum in Lisle, Illinois. Her contributions to the field have been recognized by the Garden Club, the Audubon Society, and the American Horticultural Society. In addition to having written and edited books for the Nature Study Guild, she is the author of *Reading The Landscape* and *Reading The Landscape of Europe.*

Tom Watts holds a Bachelor's degree in biology from North Central College, Naperville, Illinois, and has a Master's in social science from the University of Chicago. A retired instructional technologist, who has written many of the Guild's books himself, he now heads the organization his mother started and carries on her legacy—increasing the public's awareness and appreciation of plants through books.

This volume incorporates *Flower Finder, Sierra Flower Finder,* **and** *Redwood Region Flower Finder,* **originally published separately by the Nature Study Guild.**

Also from
The Nature Study Guild

Master Tree Finder

Published by
WARNER BOOKS

MASTER
FLOWER
FINDER

NATURE STUDY GUILD

WARNER BOOKS

A Warner Communications Company

CONTENTS

FLOWER FINDER

By   May Theilgaard Watts

A KEY to SPRING WILD FLOWERS and FLOWER FAMILIES
East of the Rockies and North of the Smokies,
Exclusive of Trees and Shrubs.

BOTANICAL TERMS USED IN DESCRIBING FLOWERS

anther ——— pollen-bearing part of stamen

calyx ——— outer part of flower, composed of sepals, usually green

corolla ——— part of flower between calyx and stamens, composed of petals

filament ——— stem of stamen

head ——— compact mass of small stemless flowers

Involucre ——— leafy growth encircling head or cluster

Irregular (flower) ——— having petals of different sizes and shapes

ovary ——— lower, enlarged part of pistil

Inferior (ovary) ——— ovary united with the calyx

superior (ovary) ——— ovary having calyx and corolla inserted at its base

petal ——— one division of corolla

pistil ——— seed-bearing central part of flower

polypetalous ——— having separate petals

regular ——— having petals all of about same size and shape

sepal ——— one division of calyx

stamen ——— pollen-bearing part, composed of anther and filament

stigma ——— sticky part of pistil which receives pollen

style ——— neck of pistil, between stigma and ovary

sympetalous ——— having petals more or less united (one cannot be removed without tearing others)

umbel ——— cluster with stems arising from one point

alternate —— coming out singly along stem

basal —— growing on the ground at foot of plant

compound —— made up of leaflets

entire —— margin without teeth or lobes

leaflet —— leaf-like part of a compound leaf

lobed —— with deeply indented margin

net-veined —— veins branching from midrib

opposite —— having two leaves coming at same level

palmately compound —— having leaflets coming from one point

parallel veins —— veins running side by side from base to tip of leaf

perfoliate —— having base surrounding stem

pinnately compound —— having leaflets not all from one point

pubescent —— covered with soft hair

sessile —— without a stem

simple —— not made up of leaflets

stipule —— small leaf-like growth at base of stem

toothed —— margin with edge like a saw

whorled —— having several leaves from one level on stem

1. Start at the beginning (below).
2. Choose the description that fits the flower to be identified.
3. Proceed to the symbol 🔲 indicated, on the page indicated.
   4. Continue in this manner through the key until the flower is located in its family.
      5. Continue within the family to the name and picture of your flower.

START HERE

If the flowering part is composed of a modified leaf surrounding a spike bearing tiny flowers   Go on page 4 to the **ARUM FAMILY**

If what looks like a flower is a mass of tightly-packed, stemless, small flowers with 2-parted stigmas; and this mass is surrounded by a green, leafy growth   Go on page 58 to the **COMPOSITE FAMILY**

If flowers are not on a club-like spike nor in a compact head   Go on page 5 to

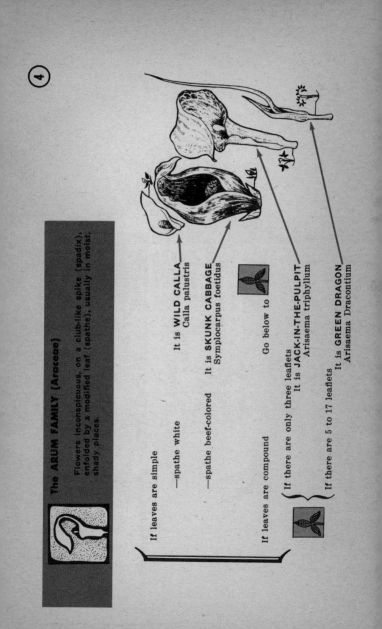

The ARUM FAMILY (Araceae)

Flowers inconspicuous, on a club-like spike (spadix), enfolded by a modified leaf (spathe), usually in moist, shady places.

If leaves are simple

—spathe white   It is WILD CALLA
                           Calla palustris

—spathe beef-colored   It is SKUNK CABBAGE
                               Symplocarpus foetidus

If leaves are compound   Go below to

If there are only three leaflets
              It is JACK-IN-THE-PULPIT
                     Arisaema triphyllum

If there are 5 to 17 leaflets
              It is GREEN DRAGON
                     Arisaema Dracontium

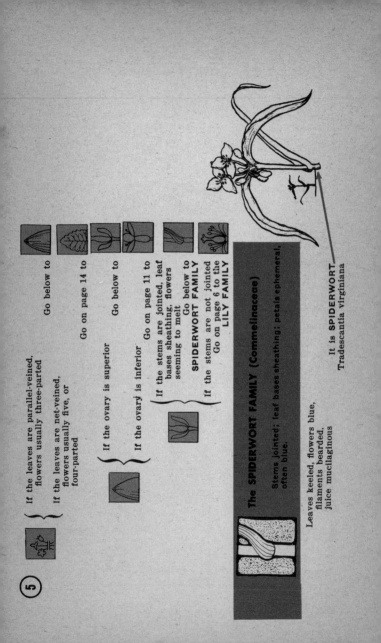

If the leaves are parallel-veined, flowers usually three-parted — Go below to

If the leaves are net-veined, flowers usually five, or four-parted — Go on page 14 to

If the ovary is superior — Go below to

If the ovary is inferior — Go on page 11 to

If the stems are jointed, leaf bases sheathing, flowers seeming to melt — Go below to SPIDERWORT FAMILY

If the stems are not jointed — Go on page 6 to the LILY FAMILY

The SPIDERWORT FAMILY (Commelinaceae)

Stems jointed; leaf bases sheathing; petals ephemeral, often blue.

Leaves keeled, flowers blue, filaments bearded, juice mucilaginous

It is SPIDERWORT
Tradescantia virginiana

The LILY FAMILY (Liliaceae)

Flower parts in threes; stamens six; leaves parallel-veined; ovary superior, 3-celled.

If the sepals and petals are different in color   Go below to

If the sepals and petals are of the same color   Go on page 7 to

—petals red or purple   It is **WAKE ROBIN (PRAIRIE TRILLIUM)**
Trillium recurvatum

—petals white on plants not more than 6" high, blooming very early   It is **DWARF TRILLIUM**
Trillium nivale

—petals white, plants taller
—flowers inverted   It is **SHY TRILLIUM**
Trillium flexipes

—flowers upright
—without purple stripes   It is **WHITE TRILLIUM**
Trillium grandiflorum

—with purple stripes at base   It is **PAINTED TRILLIUM**
Trillium undulatum

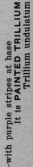

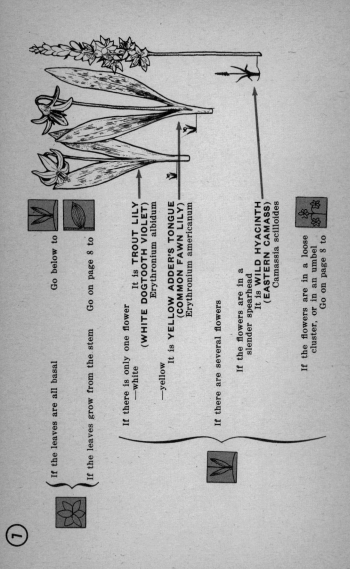

⑦

If the leaves are all basal   Go below to

If the leaves grow from the stem   Go on page 8 to

If there is only one flower

  —white   It is TROUT LILY
       (WHITE DOGTOOTH VIOLET)
           Erythronium albidum

  —yellow
     It is YELLOW ADDER'S TONGUE
      (COMMON FAWN LILY)
       Erythronium americanum

If there are several flowers

   If the flowers are in a
     slender spearhead
      It is WILD HYACINTH
      (EASTERN CAMASS)
       Camassia scilloides

   If the flowers are in a loose
     cluster, or in an umbel
       Go on page 8 to

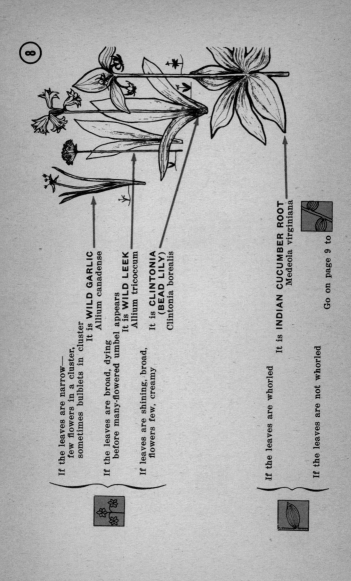

If the leaves are narrow—
few flowers in a cluster,
sometimes bulblets in cluster

It is **WILD GARLIC**
Allium canadense

If the leaves are broad, dying
before many-flowered umbel appears

It is **WILD LEEK**
Allium tricoccum

If leaves are shining, broad,
flowers few, creamy

It is **CLINTONIA**
(BEAD LILY)
Clintonia borealis

If the leaves are whorled   It is **INDIAN CUCUMBER ROOT**
Medeola virginiana

If the leaves are not whorled

Go on page 9 to

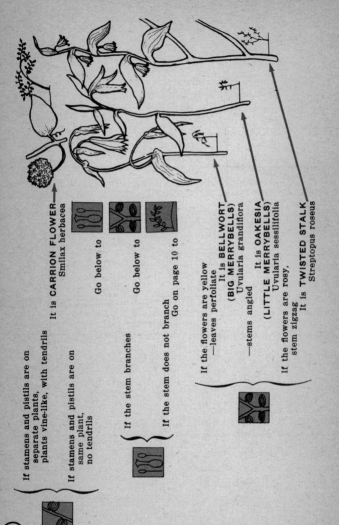

If stamens and pistils are on
separate plants,
plants vine-like, with tendrils
                It is **CARRION FLOWER** ➤
                    Smilax herbacea

                    Go below to

If stamens and pistils are on
same plant,
no tendrils

        If the stem branches
                    Go below to

        If the stem does not branch
                    Go on page 10 to

If the flowers are yellow
    —leaves perfoliate
                    It is **BELLWORT**
                    (BIG MERRYBELLS)
                        Uvularia grandiflora

    —stems angled
                    It is **OAKESIA**
                    (LITTLE MERRYBELLS)
                        Uvularia sessilifolia

If the flowers are rosy,
    stem zigzag
                    It is **TWISTED STALK**
                        Streptopus roseus

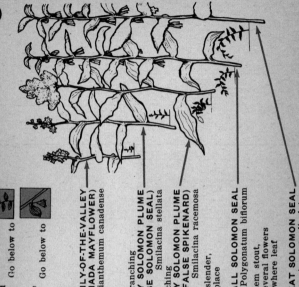

If the flowers are clustered at the end of the stalk   Go below to

If the flowers grow from place where leaf joins stem   Go below to

If flowers are 4-parted, leaf bases heart-shaped
It is **WILD LILY-OF-THE-VALLEY**
(CANADA MAYFLOWER)
Maianthemum canadense

If the flowers are 6-parted

—flower cluster not branching
It is **STARRY SOLOMON PLUME**
(FALSE SOLOMON SEAL)
Smilacina stellata

—flower cluster branching
It is **FEATHERY SOLOMON PLUME**
(FALSE SPIKENARD)
Smilacina racemosa

If the leaves are flat, stem slender, usually 2 flowers from place where leaf joins stem
It is **SMALL SOLOMON SEAL**
Polygonatum biflorum

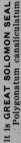

If the leaves are ruffled, stem stout, and there are usually several flowers in a cluster from place where leaf joins stem
It is **GREAT SOLOMON SEAL**
Polygonatum canaliculatum

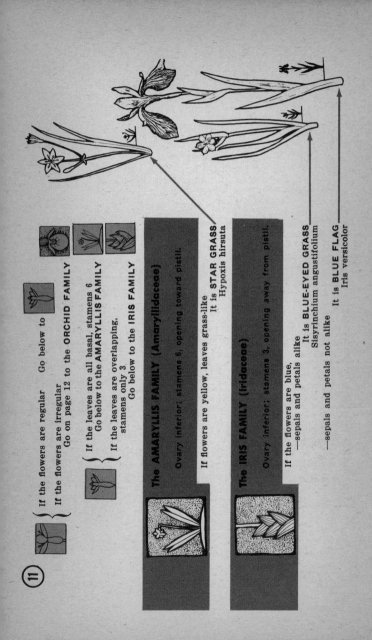

If the flowers are regular   Go below to

If the flowers are irregular
   Go on page 12 to the ORCHID FAMILY

If the leaves are all basal, stamens 6
   Go below to the AMARYLLIS FAMILY

If the leaves are overlapping,
   stamens only 3
   Go below to the IRIS FAMILY

The AMARYLLIS FAMILY (Amaryllidaceae)

Ovary inferior; stamens 6, opening toward pistil.

If flowers are yellow, leaves grass-like
   It is STAR GRASS
   Hypoxis hirsuta

The IRIS FAMILY (Iridaceae)

Ovary inferior; stamens 3, opening away from pistil.

If the flowers are blue,
  —sepals and petals alike
   It is BLUE-EYED GRASS
   Sisyrinchium angustifolium

  —sepals and petals not alike
   It is BLUE FLAG
   Iris versicolor

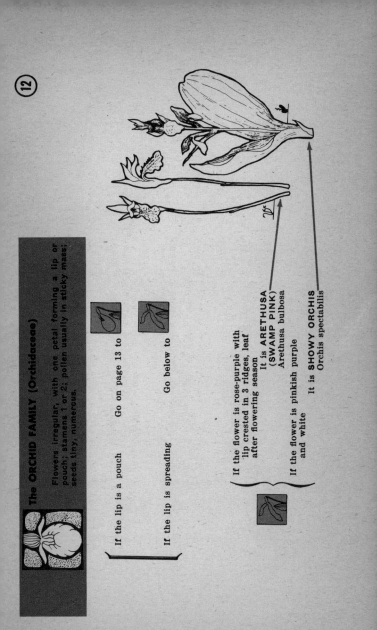

The ORCHID FAMILY (Orchidaceae)

Flowers irregular, with one petal forming a lip or pouch; stamens 1 or 2; pollen usually in sticky mass; seeds tiny, numerous.

If the lip is a pouch   Go on page 13 to

If the lip is spreading   Go below to

If the flower is rose-purple with lip crested in 3 ridges, leaf after flowering season
    It is **ARETHUSA (SWAMP PINK)**
    Arethusa bulbosa

If the flower is pinkish purple and white
    It is **SHOWY ORCHIS**
    Orchis spectabilis

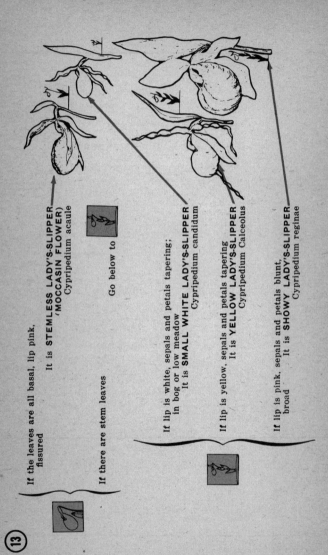

If the leaves are all basal, lip pink,
fissured

It is **STEMLESS LADY'S-SLIPPER**
('MOCCASIN FLOWER)
Cypripedium acaule

Go below to

If there are stem leaves

If lip is white, sepals and petals tapering;
in bog or low meadow
It is **SMALL WHITE LADY'S-SLIPPER**
Cypripedium candidum

If lip is yellow, sepals and petals tapering
It is **YELLOW LADY'S-SLIPPER**
Cypripedium Calceolus

If lip is pink, sepals and petals blunt,
broad   It is **SHOWY LADY'S-SLIPPER**
Cypripedium reginae

If the flowers have numerous stamens (usually more than 12)
Go below to

If the flowers have few stamens (rarely more than twice as many as petals or sepals)
Go on page 22 to

If the stamens are united by their filaments into a sheath around the pistil, the whole forming a club-like center
Go on page 20 to the **MALLOW FAMILY**

If stamens are not united

If the sepals are united at the base, and petals and stamens are attached to calyx tube
Go on page 21 to the **ROSE FAMILY**

If the sepals are not united; and stamens, sepals, petals, and pistil (or pistils) are, all unconnected
Go on page 15 to

(15)

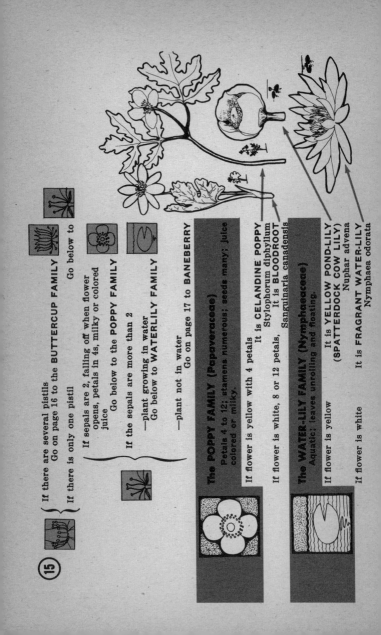

If there are several pistils
　　Go on page 16 to the BUTTERCUP FAMILY

If there is only one pistil
　　　　　　　　　　　　　　　Go below to

If sepals are 2, falling off when flower
opens, petals in 4s, milky or colored
juice
　　Go below to the POPPY FAMILY

If the sepals are more than 2

　—plant growing in water
　　Go below to WATERLILY FAMILY

　—plant not in water
　　Go on page 17 to BANEBERRY

The POPPY FAMILY (Papaveraceae)
Petals 4 to 12; stamens numerous; seeds many; juice
colored or milky.

If flower is yellow with 4 petals
　　　　　　　It is CELANDINE POPPY
　　　　　　　　　Stylophorum diphyllum

If flower is white, 8 or 12 petals,　It is BLOODROOT
　　　　　　　　　　Sanguinaria canadensis

The WATER-LILY FAMILY (Nymphaeaceae)
Aquatic; leaves unrolling and floating.

If flower is yellow　　　It is YELLOW POND-LILY
　　　　　　　　　　(SPATTERDOCK COW LILY)
　　　　　　　　　　　　Nuphar advena

If flower is white　　It is FRAGRANT WATER-LILY
　　　　　　　　　　　Nymphaea odorata

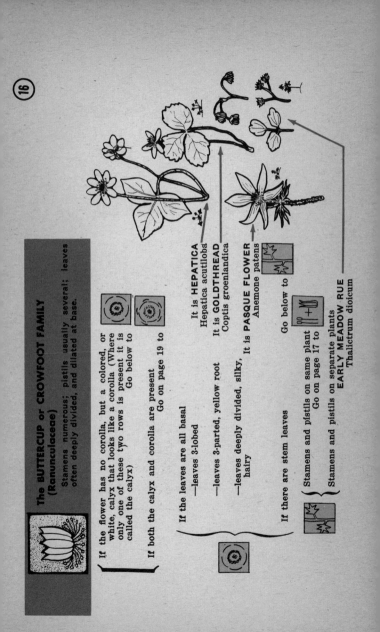

The BUTTERCUP or CROWFOOT FAMILY (Ranunculaceae)

Stamens numerous; pistils usually several; leaves often deeply divided, and dilated at base.

If the flower has no corolla, but a colored, or white, calyx that looks like a corolla (Where only one of these two rows is present it is called the calyx)
Go below to

If both the calyx and corolla are present
Go on page 19 to

If the leaves are all basal

—leaves 3-lobed
It is HEPATICA
Hepatica acutiloba

—leaves 3-parted, yellow root
It is GOLDTHREAD
Coptis groenlandica

—leaves deeply divided, silky, hairy
It is PASQUE FLOWER
Anemone patens

If there are stem leaves
Go below to

Stamens and pistils on same plant
Go on page 17 to

Stamens and pistils on separate plants
EARLY MEADOW RUE
Thalictrum dioicum

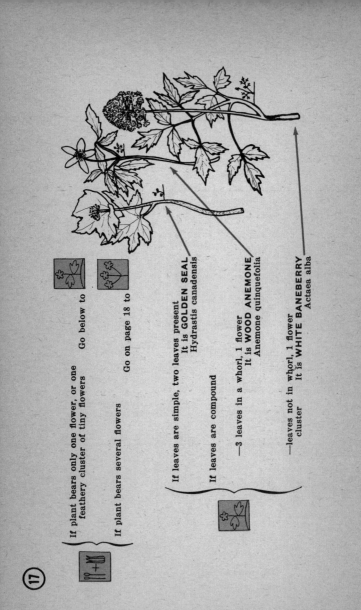

If plant bears only one flower, or one
feathery cluster of tiny flowers   Go below to

If plant bears several flowers   Go on page 18 to

{

If leaves are simple, two leaves present
It is **GOLDEN SEAL**
Hydrastis canadensis

If leaves are compound

  —3 leaves in a whorl, 1 flower
It is **WOOD ANEMONE**
Anemone quinquefolia

  —leaves not in whorl, 1 flower
cluster   It is **WHITE BANEBERRY**
Actaea alba

}

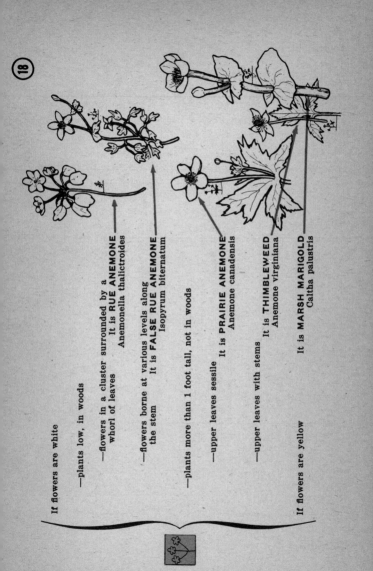

If flowers are white

—plants low, in woods

—flowers in a cluster surrounded by a whorl of leaves
It is **RUE ANEMONE**
Anemonella thalictroides

—flowers borne at various levels along the stem
It is **FALSE RUE ANEMONE**
Isopyrum biternatum

—plants more than 1 foot tall, not in woods

—upper leaves sessile
It is **PRAIRIE ANEMONE**
Anemone canadensis

—upper leaves with stems
It is **THIMBLEWEED**
Anemone virginiana

It is **MARSH MARIGOLD**
Caltha palustris

If flowers are yellow

If the flowers are yellow

—with petals tiny, inconspicuous
It is **SMALL-FLOWERED BUTTERCUP**
Ranunculus abortivus

—with petals showy

—petals rather narrow, leaflets
sessile, margins lobed
It is **EARLY BUTTERCUP**
Ranunculus fascicularis

—petals broad

—leaflets deeply toothed
It is **SWAMP BUTTERCUP**
Ranunculus septentrionalis

—leaves deeply slashed, stems hairy
It is **TALL BUTTERCUP**
Ranunculus acris

If flowers are red and yellow, inverted
It is **AMERICAN COLUMBINE**
Aquilegia canadensis

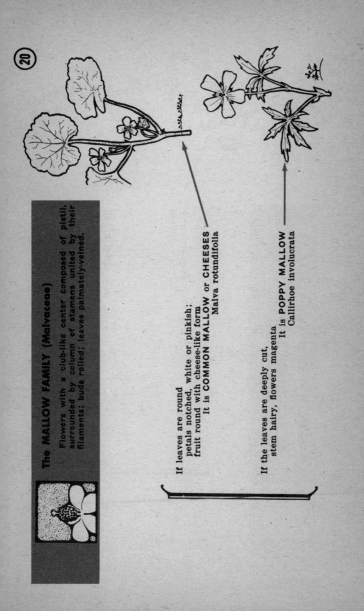

The MALLOW FAMILY (Malvaceae)

Flowers with a club-like center composed of pistil, surrounded by column of stamens united by their filaments; buds rolled; leaves palmately-veined.

If leaves are round
petals notched, white or pinkish;
fruit round with cheese-like form
It is COMMON MALLOW or CHEESES
Malva rotundifolia

If the leaves are deeply cut,
stem hairy, flowers magenta
It is POPPY MALLOW
Callirhoe involucrata

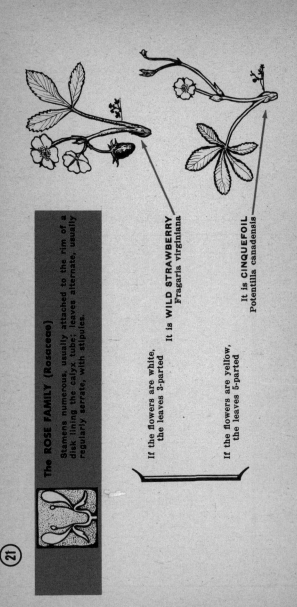

The ROSE FAMILY (Rosaceae)

Stamens numerous, usually attached to the rim of a disk lining the calyx tube; leaves alternate, usually regularly serrate, with stipules.

If the flowers are white, the leaves 3-parted

It is WILD STRAWBERRY
Fragaria virginiana

If the flowers are yellow, the leaves 5-parted

It is CINQUEFOIL
Potentilla canadensis

If the flowers are polypetalous (one petal may be pulled off without tearing any others)   Go below to

 If the flowers are sympetalous (petals joined along their sides)   Go on page 45 to

If the flower is 4-parted or 2-parted   Go on page 23 to

If the flower is 5-parted   Go on page 27 to

If the flower is 6 to 9 parted with 6 to 9 stamens opposite the petals; stamens opening by hinges at top   Go on page 23 to **BARBERRY FAMILY**

If the flower is 3-parted, without petals, sepals 3, mahogany-colored, united with ovary, stamens 6 or 12
    It is **WILD GINGER**
Asarum canadense
(BIRTHWORT FAMILY, Aristolochaceae)

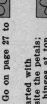

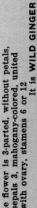

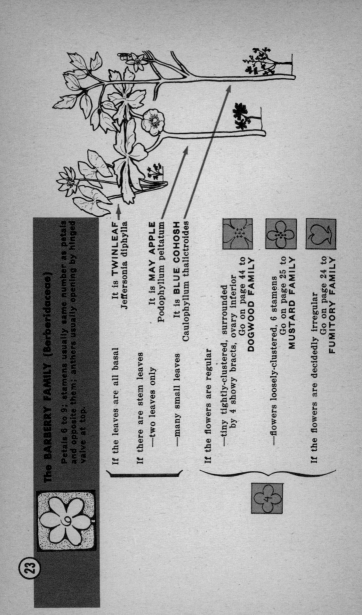

The BARBERRY FAMILY (Berberidaceae)

Petals 6 to 9; stamens usually same number as petals and opposite them; anthers usually opening by hinged valve at top.

If the leaves are all basal   It is TWINLEAF
                                           Jeffersonia diphylla

If there are stem leaves

    —two leaves only   It is MAY APPLE
                                   Podophyllum peltatum

    —many small leaves   It is BLUE COHOSH
                                 Caulophyllum thalictroides

If the flowers are regular

    —tiny tightly-clustered, surrounded
       by 4 showy bracts, ovary inferior
                 Go on page 44 to
                 DOGWOOD FAMILY

    —flowers loosely-clustered, 6 stamens
                 Go on page 25 to
                 MUSTARD FAMILY

If the flowers are decidedly irregular
                 Go on page 24 to
                 FUMITORY FAMILY

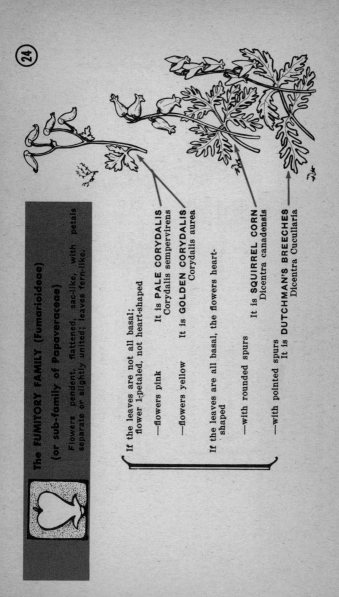

The FUMITORY FAMILY (Fumarioideae)
(or sub-family of Papaveraceae)

Flowers pendent, flattened, sac-like, with petals separate or slightly united; leaves fern-like.

If the leaves are not all basal;
flower 1-petaled, not heart-shaped

—flowers pink   It is **PALE CORYDALIS**
                    Corydalis sempervirens

—flowers yellow   It is **GOLDEN CORYDALIS**
                    Corydalis aurea

If the leaves are all basal, the flowers heart-
shaped

—with rounded spurs   It is **SQUIRREL CORN**
                        Dicentra canadensis

—with pointed spurs
                    It is **DUTCHMAN'S BREECHES**
                        Dicentra Cucullaria

The MUSTARD FAMILY (Cruciferae)

Juice pungent; flower with 4 petals, 4 sepals, and 6 stamens (4 long, 2 short); fruit 2-parted with thin partition.

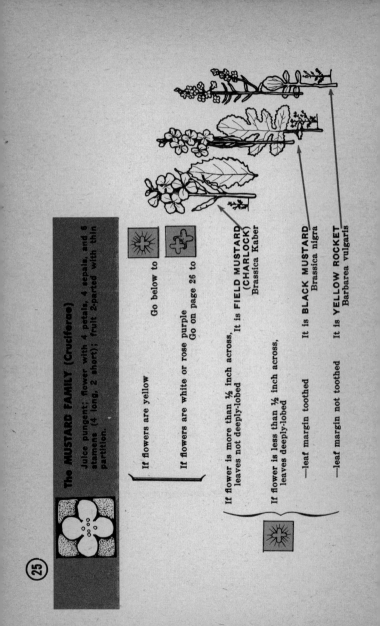

If flowers are yellow — Go below to

If flowers are white or rose purple — Go on page 26 to

If flower is more than ½ inch across, leaves not deeply-lobed — It is FIELD MUSTARD (CHARLOCK) Brassica Kaber

If flower is less than ½ inch across, leaves deeply-lobed

—leaf margin toothed — It is BLACK MUSTARD Brassica nigra

—leaf margin not toothed — It is YELLOW ROCKET Barbarea vulgaris

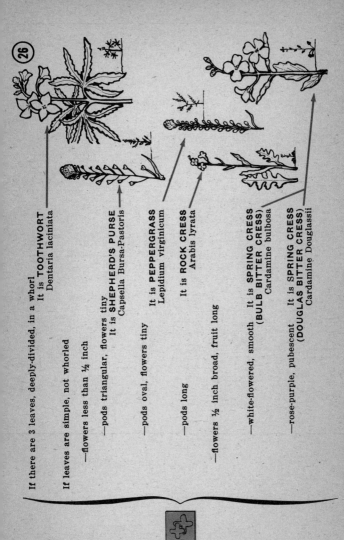

If there are 3 leaves, deeply-divided, in a whorl
It is **TOOTHWORT**
Dentaria laciniata

If leaves are simple, not whorled

—flowers less than ½ inch

—pods triangular, flowers tiny
It is **SHEPHERD'S PURSE**
Capsella Bursa-Pastoris

—pods oval, flowers tiny   It is **PEPPERGRASS**
Lepidium virginicum

—pods long   It is **ROCK CRESS**
Arabis lyrata

—flowers ½ inch broad, fruit long

—white-flowered, smooth   It is **SPRING CRESS**
(**BULB BITTER CRESS**)
Cardamine bulbosa

—rose-purple, pubescent   It is **SPRING CRESS**
(**DOUGLAS BITTER CRESS**)
Cardamine Douglassii

If the flower is regular
(having petals all of the same size and shape)
Go below to

If the flower is irregular
(having petals of different shapes)
Go on page 32 to

If ovary is superior
(Ovary is entirely within the
flower and can be removed
without tearing the calyx or
corolla)   Go below to

If ovary is not superior   Go below to

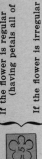

If the leaves are simple
Go on page 28 to

If the leaves are compound
Go on page 39 to
OXALIS FAMILY

If the leaves are basal
(or all but 2 are basal);
ovary partly inferior
Go on page 40 to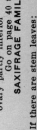
SAXIFRAGE FAMILY

If there are stem leaves;
flowers many, in clusters
Go on page 41 to

27

If flowers have 5 sepals   Go on page 29 to

If flowers have 2 sepals, fleshy leaves
Go below to **PORTULACA FAMILY**

The PORTULACA or PURSLANE FAMILY
(Portulacaceae)

Leaves succulent; flowers open only in sunshine;
stamens usually 5 and opposite petals; 2 sepals.

If the leaves are narrow,   It is **SPRING BEAUTY**
    grass-like   Claytonia virginica

If the leaves are entire;
joints of stem swollen
Go on page 30 to PINK FAMILY

If the leaves are deeply-lobed
Go below to GERANIUM FAMILY

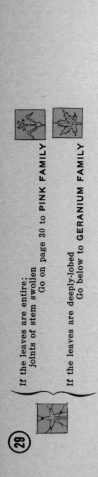

The GERANIUM FAMILY (Geraniaceae)

Leaves deeply-lobed; stems soft; stamens 10; styles
5-parted.

If flower is 1" or more across;
leaves somewhat circular in outline:
stem usually unbranched   It is **WILD GERANIUM**
(CRANESBILL)
Geranium maculatum

If flower is ½" or less across; stems much branched
—flowers in a close cluster
It is **CAROLINA CRANESBILL**
Geranium carolinianum

—flowers not in close clusters;
stems ruddy; with strong odor
It is **HERB ROBERT**
Geranium Robertianum

The PINK FAMILY (Caryophyllaceae)

Leaves opposite, entire, often united at base; stems usually swollen at joints; sepals 5; styles 2 to 5.

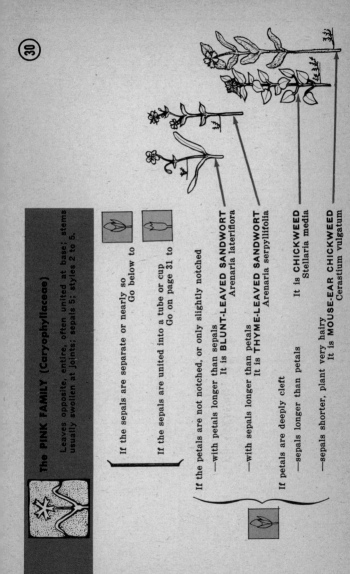

If the sepals are separate or nearly so
　　　　　　　　　　　　　Go below to

If the sepals are united into a tube or cup
　　　　　　　　　　　　　Go on page 31 to

If the petals are not notched, or only slightly notched
—with petals longer than sepals
　　　　It is **BLUNT-LEAVED SANDWORT**
　　　　　　　　　　　　Arenaria lateriflora

—with sepals longer than petals
　　　　It is **THYME-LEAVED SANDWORT**
　　　　　　　　　　　　Arenaria serpyllifolia

If petals are deeply cleft
—sepals longer than petals
　　　　It is **CHICKWEED**
　　　　　　　　　　　　Stellaria media

—sepals shorter, plant very hairy
　　　　It is **MOUSE-EAR CHICKWEED**
　　　　　　　　　　　　Cerastium vulgatum

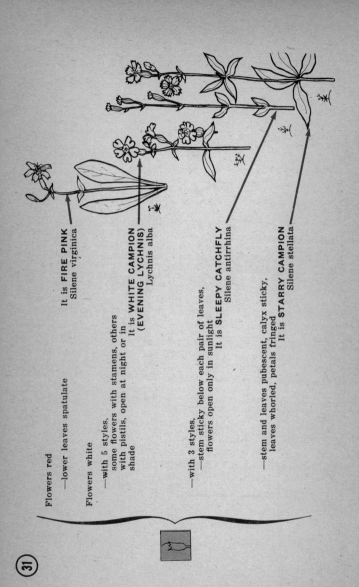

Flowers red
—lower leaves spatulate
       It is **FIRE PINK**
          Silene virginica

Flowers white

—with 5 styles,
  some flowers with stamens, others
  with pistils, open at night or in
  shade
      It is **WHITE CAMPION**
      (EVENING LYCHNIS)
         Lychnis alba

—with 3 styles,
  —stem sticky below each pair of leaves,
    flowers open only in sunlight
      It is **SLEEPY CATCHFLY**
        Silene antirrhina

  —stem and leaves pubescent, calyx sticky,
    leaves whorled, petals fringed
      It is **STARRY CAMPION**
        Silene stellata

If the colored parts of the flower are 3,
stamens united to each other and to petals
Go on page 33 to **MILKWORT FAMILY**

Go below to

If there are 5 petals

If there are 5 stamens;
the lower petal marked with lines
Go on page 34 to **VIOLET FAMILY**

If there are 10 stamens;
2 petals forming a keel
Go on page 36 to **LEGUME FAMILY**

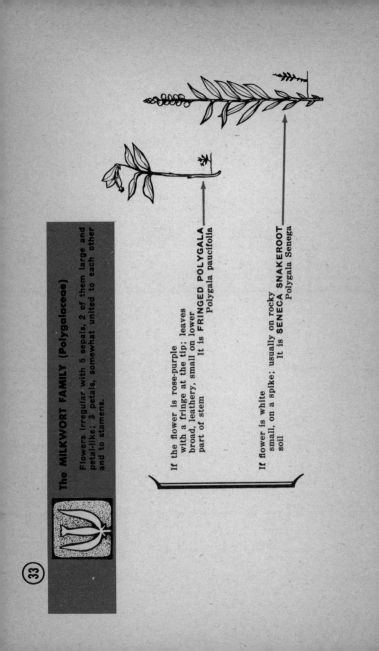

33

The MILKWORT FAMILY (Polygalaceae)

Flowers irregular with 5 sepals, 2 of them large and petal-like; 3 petals, somewhat united to each other and to stamens.

If the flower is rose-purple
with a fringe at the tip; leaves
broad, leathery, small on lower
part of stem   It is **FRINGED POLYGALA**
Polygala paucifolia

If flower is white
small, on a spike; usually on rocky
soil   It is **SENECA SNAKEROOT**
Polygala Senega

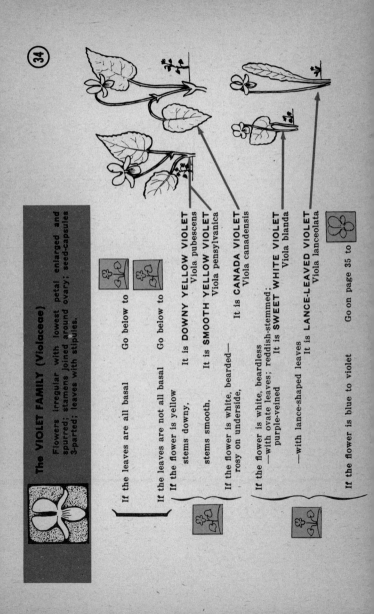

The VIOLET FAMILY (Violaceae)

Flowers irregular with lowest petal enlarged and spurred; stamens joined around ovary; seed-capsules 3-parted; leaves with stipules.

If the leaves are all basal   Go below to

If the leaves are not all basal   Go below to

If the flower is yellow

stems downy,   It is **DOWNY YELLOW VIOLET**
Viola pubescens

stems smooth,   It is **SMOOTH YELLOW VIOLET**
Viola pensylvanica

If the flower is white, bearded——   It is **CANADA VIOLET**
rosy on underside,   Viola canadensis

If the flower is white, beardless
—with ovate leaves; reddish-stemmed;
purple-veined   It is **SWEET WHITE VIOLET**
Viola blanda

—with lance-shaped leaves
It is **LANCE-LEAVED VIOLET**
Viola lanceolata

If the flower is blue to violet   Go on page 35 to

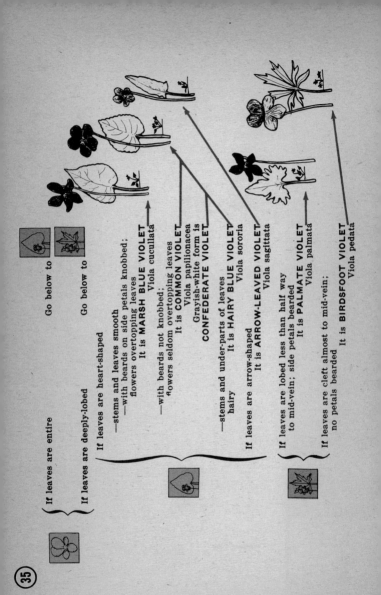

If leaves are entire   Go below to

If leaves are deeply-lobed   Go below to

If leaves are heart-shaped

—stems and leaves smooth
  —with beards on side petals knobbed;
    flowers overtopping leaves
      It is **MARSH BLUE VIOLET**
          Viola cucullata

  —with beards not knobbed;
    flowers seldom overtopping leaves
      It is **COMMON VIOLET**
          Viola papilionacea
      Grayish-white form is
      CONFEDERATE VIOLET

—stems and under-parts of leaves
  hairy   It is **HAIRY BLUE VIOLET**
          Viola sororia

If leaves are arrow-shaped
      It is **ARROW-LEAVED VIOLET**
          Viola sagittata

If leaves are lobed less than half way
  to mid-vein; side petals bearded
      It is **PALMATE VIOLET**
          Viola palmata

If leaves are cleft almost to mid-vein;
  no petals bearded
      It is **BIRDSFOOT VIOLET**
          Viola pedata

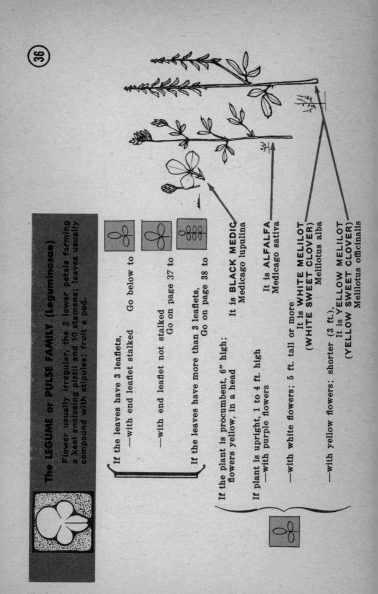

The LEGUME or PULSE FAMILY (Leguminosae)

Flower usually irregular, the 2 lower petals forming a keel enclosing pistil and 10 stamens; leaves usually compound with stipules; fruit a pod.

If the leaves have 3 leaflets,
—with end leaflet stalked   Go below to

—with end leaflet not stalked
Go on page 37 to

If the leaves have more than 3 leaflets,
Go on page 38 to

If the plant is procumbent, 6" high; flowers yellow, in a head   It is **BLACK MEDIC**
Medicago lupulina

If plant is upright, 1 to 4 ft. high
—with purple flowers   It is **ALFALFA**
Medicago sativa

—with white flowers; 5 ft. tall or more
It is **WHITE MELILOT**
(WHITE SWEET CLOVER)
Melilotus alba

—with yellow flowers; shorter (3 ft.),
It is **YELLOW MELILOT**
(YELLOW SWEET CLOVER)
Melilotus officinalis

If the flowers in the head are stalked, leaves smooth;

— white to pinkish flowers; creeping plant;
  leaflets indented at tip, marked with
  indistinct triangle　　It is **WHITE CLOVER**
  　　　　　　　　　　　Trifolium repens

— pinkish flowers; erect plant; leaflets with
  rounded tips, no triangle　It is **ALSIKE CLOVER**
  　　　　　　　　　　　　Trifolium hybridum

If the flowers in the head are sessile, roseate;
  leaves hairy; distinct triangle　It is **RED CLOVER**
  　　　　　　　　　　　　　　Trifolium pratense

If leaves are palmately-compound

It is **LUPINE**
Lupinus perennis

If leaves are pinnately-compound, tipped with
tendrils; plants trailing or climbing   Go below to

If leaves are thick, prominently-
veined; back and side petals curved
upward; flowers purple   It is **WILD PEA**
Lathyrus venosus

If leaves are thin; side petals joined to keel
—plants smooth

—flowers 4 to 8, purple, ¾ in. long
It is **AMERICAN VETCH**
Vicia americana

—flowers 10 or more, pale tip of
keel bluish   It is **WOOD VETCH**
Vicia caroliniana

—plant hairy, in mats; flowers many,
It is **HAIRY VETCH**
Vicia villosa

39

The OXALIS or WOOD-SORREL FAMILY (Oxalidaceae)

Juice sour; leaves with 3-notched leaflets; pod cylindric.

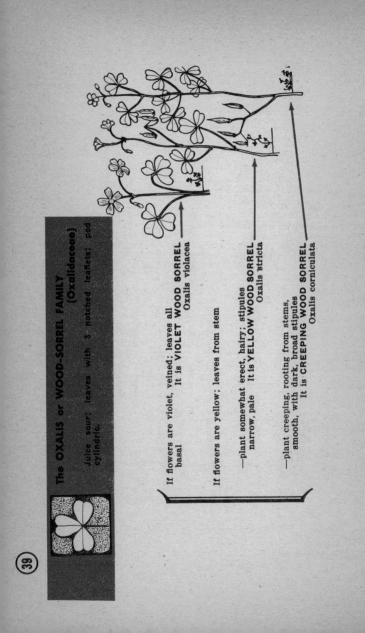

If flowers are violet, veined; leaves all basal   It is **VIOLET WOOD SORREL**
Oxalis violacea

If flowers are yellow; leaves from stem

—plant somewhat erect, hairy; stipules narrow, pale   It is **YELLOW WOOD SORREL**
Oxalis stricta

—plant creeping, rooting from stems, smooth, with dark, broad stipules   It is **CREEPING WOOD SORREL**
Oxalis corniculata

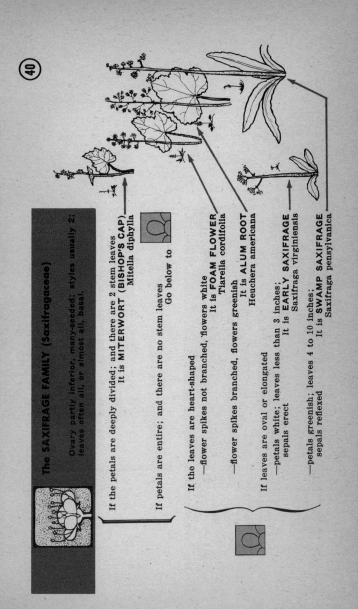

The SAXIFRAGE FAMILY (Saxifragaceae)

Ovary partly inferior, many-seeded; styles usually 2; leaves often all, or almost all, basal.

If the petals are deeply divided; and there are 2 stem leaves
It is MITERWORT (BISHOP'S CAP)
Mitella diphylla

If petals are entire; and there are no stem leaves
Go below to

If the leaves are heart-shaped
—flower spikes not branched, flowers white
It is FOAM FLOWER
Tiarella cordifolia

—flower spikes branched, flowers greenish
It is ALUM ROOT
Heuchera americana

If leaves are oval or elongated
—petals white; leaves less than 3 inches;
sepals erect
It is EARLY SAXIFRAGE
Saxifraga virginiensis

—petals greenish; leaves 4 to 10 inches;
sepals reflexed
It is SWAMP SAXIFRAGE
Saxifraga pensylvanica

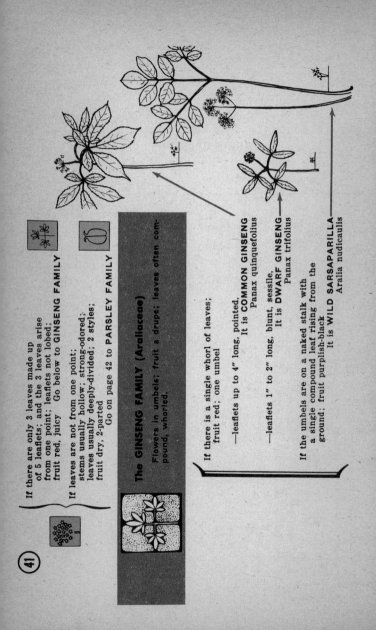

If there are only 3 leaves made up of 5 leaflets; and the 3 leaves arise from one point; leaflets not lobed; fruit red, juicy   Go below to GINSENG FAMILY

If leaves are not from one point; stems usually hollow; strong-odored; leaves usually deeply-divided; 2 styles; fruit dry, 2-parted
Go on page 42 to PARSLEY FAMILY

The GINSENG FAMILY (Araliaceae)

Flowers in umbels; fruit a drupe; leaves often compound, whorled.

If there is a single whorl of leaves; fruit red; one umbel

—leaflets up to 4" long, pointed,
It is COMMON GINSENG
Panax quinquefolius

—leaflets 1" to 2" long, blunt, sessile,
It is DWARF GINSENG
Panax trifolius

If the umbels are on a naked stalk with a single compound leaf rising from the ground; fruit purplish-black
It is WILD SARSAPARILLA
Aralia nudicaulis

The PARSLEY FAMILY (Umbelliferae)

Flowers in umbels; styles 2, ovary inferior; leaves usually compound with sheathing bases.

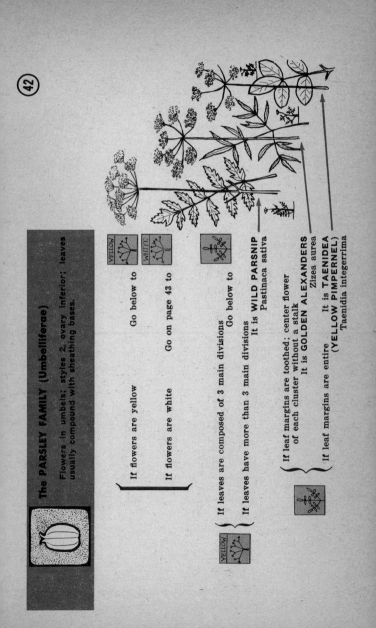

If flowers are yellow   Go below to

If flowers are white   Go on page 43 to

If leaves are composed of 3 main divisions
          Go below to

If leaves have more than 3 main divisions
          It is WILD PARSNIP
          Pastinaca sativa

If leaf margins are toothed; center flower
of each cluster without a stalk
          It is GOLDEN ALEXANDERS
          Zizea aurea

If leaf margins are entire   It is TAENIDEA
          (YELLOW PIMPERNEL)
          Taenidia integerrima

43

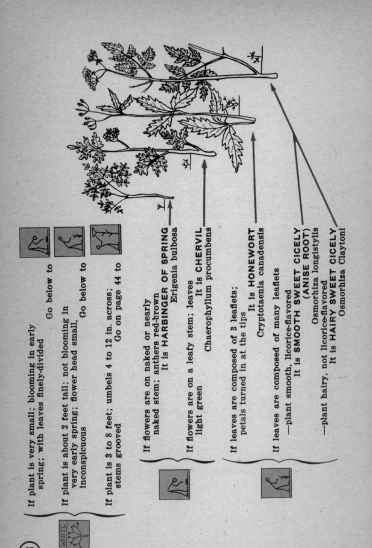

If plant is very small; blooming in early spring; with leaves finely-divided   Go below to

If plant is about 2 feet tall; not blooming in very early spring; flower head small, inconspicuous   Go below to

If plant is 3 to 8 feet; umbels 4 to 12 in. across; stems grooved   Go on page 44 to

If flowers are on naked or nearly naked stem; anthers red-brown
It is HARBINGER OF SPRING
Erigenia bulbosa

If flowers are on a leafy stem; leaves light green
It is CHERVIL
Chaerophyllum procumbens

If leaves are composed of 3 leaflets; petals turned in at the tips
It is HONEWORT
Cryptotaenia canadensis

If leaves are composed of many leaflets
—plant smooth, licorice-flavored
It is SMOOTH SWEET CICELY (ANISE ROOT)
Osmorhiza longistylis
—plant hairy, not licorice-flavored
It is HAIRY SWEET CICELY
Osmorhiza Claytoni

44

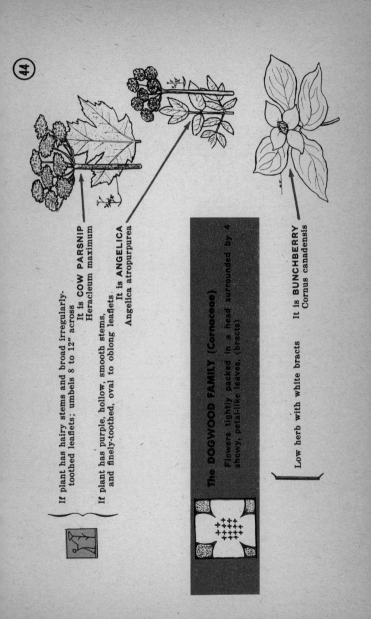

If plant has hairy stems and broad irregularly-
toothed leaflets; umbels 8 to 12" across
It is COW PARSNIP
Heracleum maximum

If plant has purple, hollow, smooth stems,
and finely-toothed, oval to oblong leaflets
It is ANGELICA
Angelica atropurpurea

The DOGWOOD FAMILY (Cornaceae)

Flowers tightly packed in a head surrounded by 4
showy, petal-like leaves, (bracts)

Low herb with white bracts   It is BUNCHBERRY
Cornus canadensis

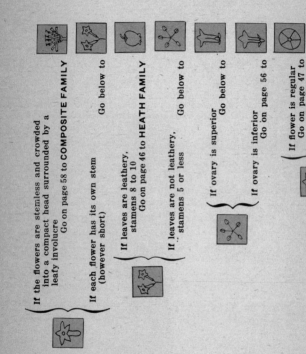

If the flowers are stemless and crowded into a compact head surrounded by a leafy involucre
Go on page 58 to COMPOSITE FAMILY

If each flower has its own stem (however short)
Go below to

If leaves are leathery, stamens 8 to 10
Go on page 46 to HEATH FAMILY

If leaves are not leathery, stamens 5 or less
Go below to

If ovary is superior
Go below to

If ovary is inferior
Go on page 56 to

If flower is regular
Go on page 47 to

If flower is irregular
Go on page 53 to

The HEATH FAMILY (Ericaceae)

Plants usually woody (these are trailing); leaves often leathery; stamens twice as many as corolla lobes, and on edge of fleshy disk; stamens opening at tips.

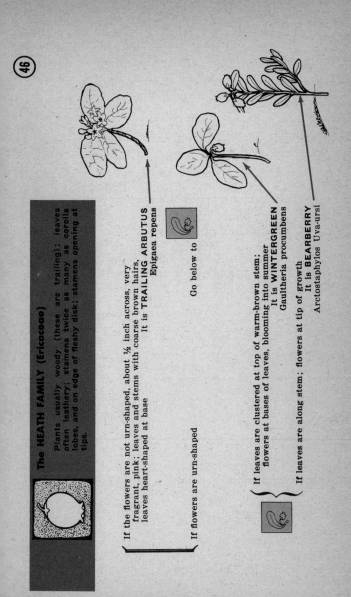

If the flowers are not urn-shaped, about ½ inch across, very fragrant, pink; leaves and stems with coarse brown hairs, leaves heart-shaped at base   It is **TRAILING ARBUTUS**
Epigaea repens

Go below to

If flowers are urn-shaped

If leaves are clustered at top of warm-brown stem; flowers at bases of leaves, blooming into summer
It is **WINTERGREEN**
Gaultheria procumbens

If leaves are along stem; flowers at tip of growth
It is **BEARBERRY**
Arctostaphylos Uva-ursi

If leaf (or leaflets), margins are entire,   Go below to

If leaf margins are toothed or lobed,   Go on page 51 to

If style is 3-lobed, pod 3-celled, Go on page 48 to
POLEMONIUM FAMILY

If style is simple,   Go below to

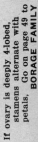

If ovary is deeply 4-lobed, stamens alternate with petals, Go on page 49 to
BORAGE FAMILY

If ovary is one-celled, stamens opposite petals, Go on page 50 to
PRIMROSE FAMILY

The POLEMONIUM or PHLOX FAMILY (Polemoniaceae)

Style 3-lobed; pod 3-celled; stamens connected to corolla tube; leaves opposite or compound; flowers clustered.

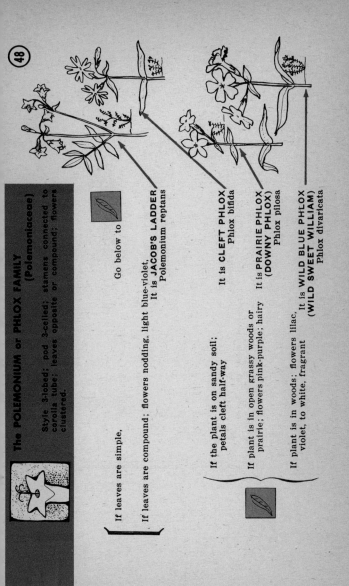

If leaves are simple,   Go below to

If leaves are compound; flowers nodding, light blue-violet,
                                         It is JACOB'S LADDER
                                              Polemonium reptans

If the plant is on sandy soil;
petals cleft half-way   It is CLEFT PHLOX
                                              Phlox bifida

If plant is in open grassy woods or
prairie; flowers pink-purple; hairy   It is PRAIRIE PHLOX
                                           (DOWNY PHLOX)
                                              Phlox pilosa

If plant is in woods; flowers lilac,
violet, to white, fragrant   It is WILD BLUE PHLOX
                                           (WILD SWEET WILLIAM)
                                              Phlox divaricata

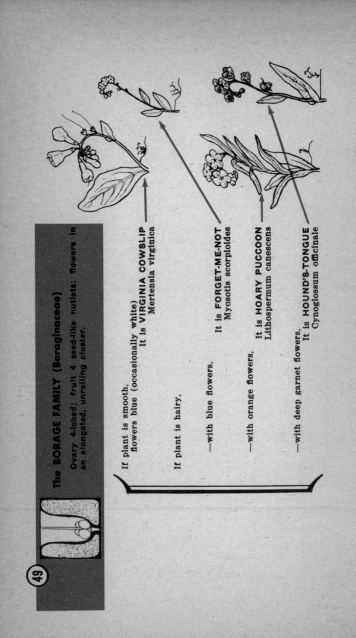

49

The BORAGE FAMILY (Boraginaceae)

Ovary 4-lobed; fruit 4 seed-like nutlets; flowers in an elongated, unrolling cluster.

If plant is smooth,
  flowers blue (occasionally white)
    It is **VIRGINIA COWSLIP**
    Mertensia virginica

If plant is hairy,

  —with blue flowers,   It is **FORGET-ME-NOT**
    Myosotis scorpioides

  —with orange flowers,   It is **HOARY PUCCOON**
    Lithospermum canescens

  —with deep garnet flowers,
    It is **HOUND'S-TONGUE**
    Cynoglossum officinale

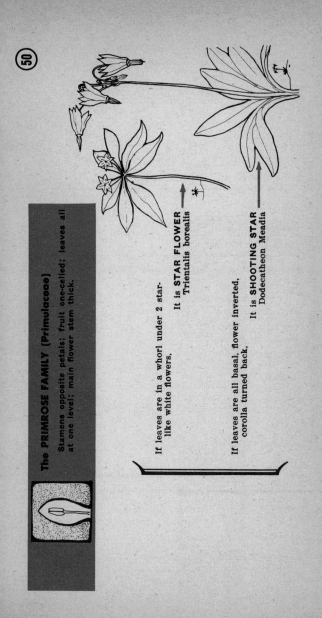

The PRIMROSE FAMILY (Primulaceae)

Stamens opposite petals; fruit one-celled; leaves all at one level; main flower stem thick.

If leaves are in a whorl under 2 star-like white flowers,

It is **STAR FLOWER**
Trientalis borealis

If leaves are all basal, flower inverted, corolla turned back,

It is **SHOOTING STAR**
Dodecatheon Meadia

If styles are 2-cleft; stamens usually loosely protruding

Go on page 52 to **WATERLEAF FAMILY**

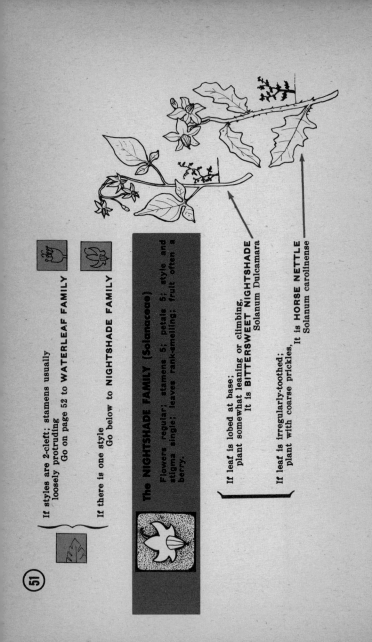

If there is one style

Go below to **NIGHTSHADE FAMILY**

The NIGHTSHADE FAMILY (Solanaceae)

Flowers regular; stamens 5; petals 5; style and stigma single; leaves rank-smelling; fruit often a berry.

If leaf is lobed at base;
plant somewhat leaning or climbing,
It is **BITTERSWEET NIGHTSHADE**
Solanum Dulcamara

If leaf is irregularly-toothed;
plant with coarse prickles,
It is **HORSE NETTLE**
Solanum carolinense

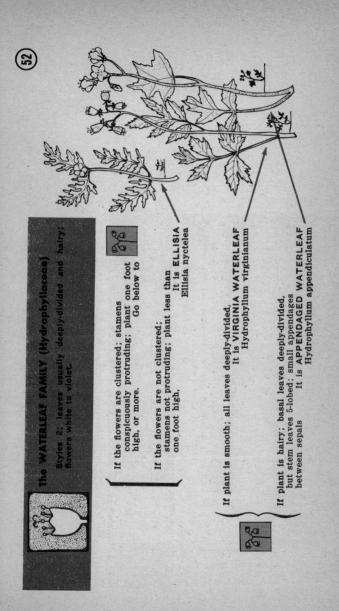

The WATERLEAF FAMILY (Hydrophyllaceae)

Styles 2; leaves usually deeply-divided and hairy; flowers white to violet.

If the flowers are clustered; stamens conspicuously protruding; plant one foot high, or more.
Go below to

It is ELLISIA
Ellisia nyctelea

If the flowers are not clustered; stamens not protruding; plant less than one foot high,

If plant is smooth; all leaves deeply-divided,
It is VIRGINIA WATERLEAF
Hydrophyllum virginianum

If plant is hairy; basal leaves deeply-divided, but stem leaves 5-lobed; small appendages between sepals
It is APPENDAGED WATERLEAF
Hydrophyllum appendiculatum

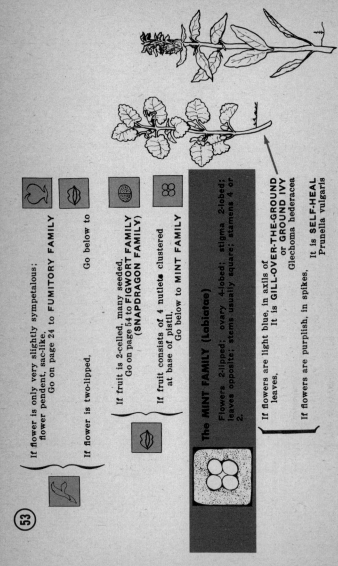

53

If flower is only very slightly sympetalous; flower pendent, sac-like,
Go on page 24 to FUMITORY FAMILY

If flower is two-lipped,
Go below to

If fruit is 2-celled, many seeded,
Go on page 54 to FIGWORT FAMILY
(SNAPDRAGON FAMILY)

If fruit consists of 4 nutlets clustered at base of pistil,
Go below to MINT FAMILY

The MINT FAMILY (Labiatae)

Flowers 2-lipped; ovary 4-lobed; stigma 2-lobed; stems usually square; stamens 4 or 2.

If flowers are light blue, in axils of leaves,
It is GILL-OVER-THE-GROUND or GROUND IVY
Glechoma hederacea

If flowers are purplish, in spikes,
It is SELF-HEAL
Prunella vulgaris

The FIGWORT FAMILY (Scrophulariaceae)

Corolla irregular, sympetalous; stamens of 2 lengths or only 2; style single; fruit a many seeded 2-cell capsule.

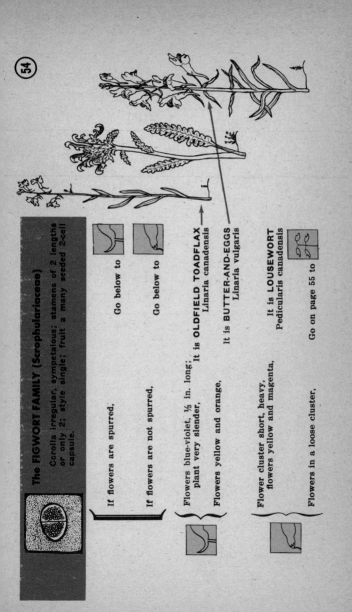

If flowers are spurred,   Go below to

If flowers are not spurred,   Go below to

Flowers blue-violet, ½ in. long; plant very slender,   It is OLDFIELD TOADFLAX
                                                                      Linaria canadensis

Flowers yellow and orange,   It is BUTTER-AND-EGGS
                                                                      Linaria vulgaris

Flower cluster short, heavy, flowers yellow and magenta,   It is LOUSEWORT
                                                                      Pedicularis canadensis

Flowers in a loose cluster,   Go on page 55 to

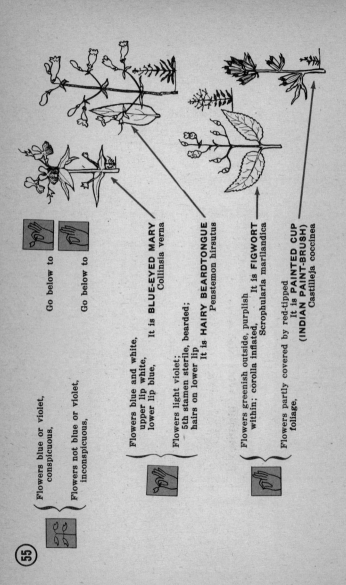

Flowers blue or violet,
conspicuous,   Go below to

Flowers not blue or violet,
inconspicuous,   Go below to

Flowers blue and white,
upper lip white,
lower lip blue,   It is **BLUE-EYED MARY**
Collinsia verna

Flowers light violet;
5th stamen sterile, bearded;
hairs on lower lip
It is **HAIRY BEARDTONGUE**
Penstemon hirsutus

Flowers greenish outside, purplish
within; corolla inflated,   It is **FIGWORT**
Scrophularia marilandica

Flowers partly covered by red-tipped
foliage,   It is **PAINTED CUP**
(INDIAN PAINT-BRUSH)
Castilleja coccinea

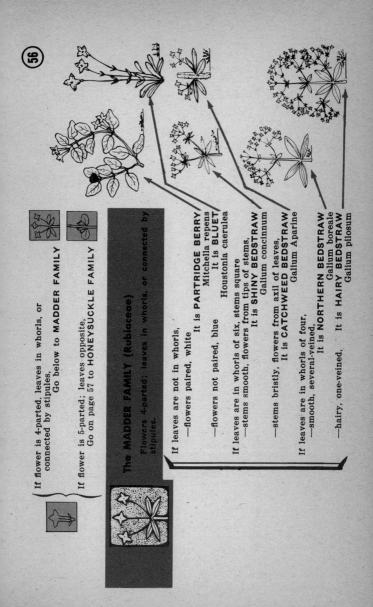

If flower is 4-parted, leaves in whorls, or connected by stipules.
   Go below to **MADDER FAMILY**

If flower is 5-parted; leaves opposite,
   Go on page 57 to **HONEYSUCKLE FAMILY**

The MADDER FAMILY (Rubiaceae)

Flowers 4-parted; leaves in whorls, or connected by stipules.

If leaves are not in whorls,
   —flowers paired, white
      It is **PARTRIDGE BERRY**
         Mitchella repens
   —flowers not paired, blue   It is **BLUET**
         Houstonia caerulea

If leaves are in whorls of six, stems square
   —stems smooth, flowers from tips of stems,
      It is **SHINY BEDSTRAW**
         Galium concinnum
   —stems bristly, flowers from axil of leaves,
      It is **CATCHWEED BEDSTRAW**
         Galium Aparine

If leaves are in whorls of four,
   —smooth, several-veined,
      It is **NORTHERN BEDSTRAW**
         Galium boreale
   —hairy, one-veined,   It is **HAIRY BEDSTRAW**
         Galium pilosum

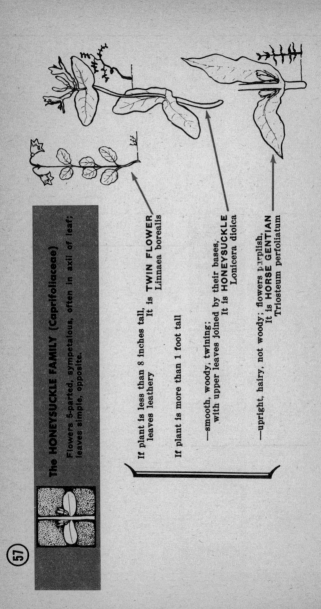

The HONEYSUCKLE FAMILY (Caprifoliaceae)

Flowers 5-parted, sympetalous, often in axil of leaf;
leaves simple, opposite.

If plant is less than 8 inches tall,
leaves leathery   It is TWIN FLOWER
                          Linnaea borealis

If plant is more than 1 foot tall

—smooth, woody, twining;
 with upper leaves joined by their bases.
                  It is HONEYSUCKLE
                      Lonicera dioica

—upright, hairy, not woody; flowers purplish.
                  It is HORSE GENTIAN
                      Triosteum perfoliatum

The COMPOSITE FAMILY (Compositae)

Flowers packed into heads, surrounded by leafy involucre; anthers united to form a tube around style; style 2-cleft at tip.

If the flowers are of 2 kinds:
tubular at center, closed-fan shape on outside, Go below to

If flowers are all closed-fan shape, Go on page 59 to

If flowers are all tubular; plant white-woolly, Go below to

It is EVERLASTING
Antennaria canadensis

It is PLANTAIN-LEAVED EVERLASTING
Antennaria plantaginifolia

It is GOLDEN RAGWORT
Senecio aureus

with small basal leaves,

with broad basal leaves,

Flowers all yellow,

Flowers not all yellow, Go on page 59 to

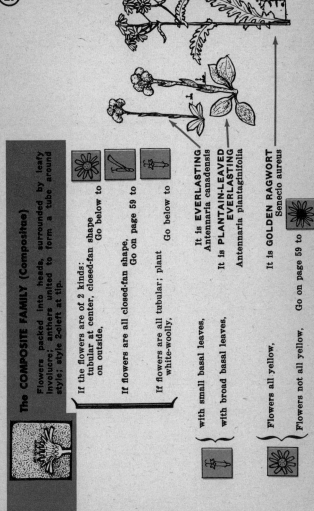

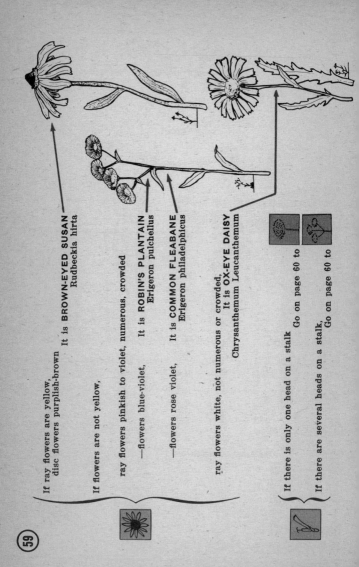

If ray flowers are yellow,
disc flowers purplish-brown   It is **BROWN-EYED SUSAN**
                                          Rudbeckia hirta

If flowers are not yellow,

   ray flowers pinkish to violet, numerous, crowded

     —flowers blue-violet,   It is **ROBIN'S PLANTAIN**
                                Erigeron pulchellus

     —flowers rose violet,   It is **COMMON FLEABANE**
                                Erigeron philadelphicus

   ray flowers white, not numerous or crowded,
                        It is **OX-EYE DAISY**
                Chrysanthemum Leucanthemum

If there is only one head on a stalk
                Go on page 60 to

If there are several heads on a stalk,
                Go on page 60 to

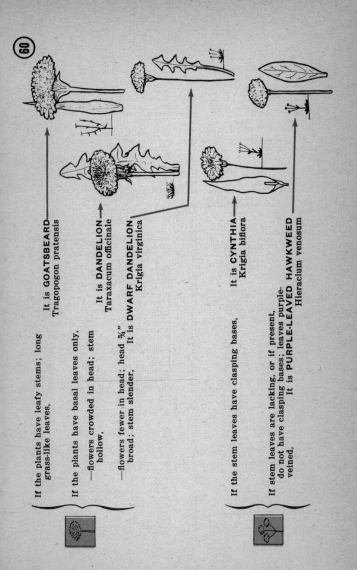

It is GOATSBEARD
Tragopogon pratensis

If the plants have leafy stems; long
grass-like leaves,

It is DANDELION
Taraxacum officinale

If the plants have basal leaves only,

—flowers crowded in head; stem
hollow,

—flowers fewer in head; head ¾"
broad; stem slender,   It is DWARF DANDELION
Krigia virginica

It is CYNTHIA
Krigia biflora

If the stem leaves have clasping bases,

If stem leaves are lacking, or if present,
do not have clasping bases; leaves purple-
veined,   It is PURPLE-LEAVED HAWKWEED
Hieracium venosum

I N D E X
to
COMMON NAMES
and
FAMILIES

Sierra Flower Finder

a guide to Sierra Nevada wildflowers

by Glenn Keator, Ph.D.
illustrated by Valerie R. Winemiller

area covered by this book

to use this book

- Find some typical leaves and flowers. It may help to look at fading flowers with developing fruits. Also note how the plant grows.

- turn to page 7, make the first choice and go on from there.

The introductory pages explain some terms you'll need and the distribution, habitat and life-zone symbols used.

This book will help you identify non-woody flowering plants (wildflowers) found in the Sierra Nevada mountain range above the foothills which end at about 4,000 feet elevation. For practical purposes, several very rare and endangered plants are excluded.

GLOSSARY

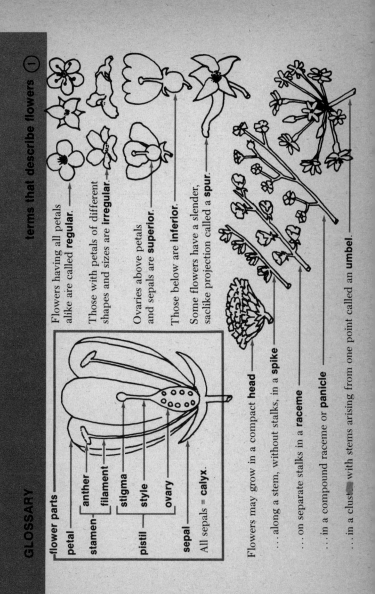

flower parts
  petal
  stamen — **anther**
       — **filament**
  pistil — **stigma**
      — **style**
      — **ovary**
  sepal

All sepals = **calyx.**

Flowers having all petals alike are called **regular.**

Those with petals of different shapes and sizes are **irregular.**

Ovaries above petals and sepals are **superior.**

Those below are **inferior.**

Some flowers have a slender, saclike projection called a **spur.**

Flowers may grow in a compact **head**

...along a stem, without stalks, in a **spike**

...on separate stalks in a **raceme**

...in a compound raceme or **panicle**

...in a cluster with stems arising from one point called an **umbel.**

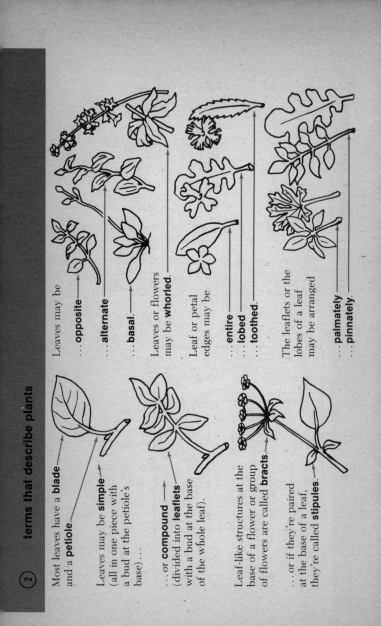

Most leaves have a **blade** and a **petiole**.

Leaves may be **simple** (all in one piece with a bud at the petiole's base)....

...or **compound** (divided into **leaflets** with a bud at the base of the whole leaf).

Leaf-like structures at the base of a flower or group of flowers are called **bracts**.

...or if they're paired at the base of a leaf, they're called **stipules**.

Leaves may be

... **opposite**

... **alternate**

... **basal**.

Leaves or flowers may be **whorled**.

Leaf or petal edges may be

... **entire**

... **lobed**

... **toothed**.

The leaflets or the lobes of a leaf may be arranged

... **palmately**

... **pinnately**.

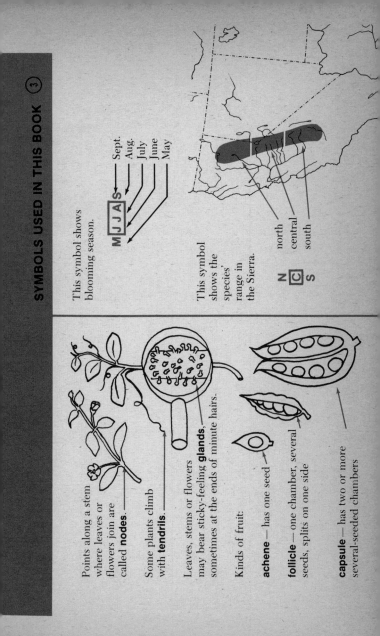

This symbol shows blooming season.

M J A S
May
June
July
Aug.
Sept.

This symbol shows the species' range in the Sierra.

N
C
S

north
central
south

Points along a stem where leaves or flowers join are called **nodes.**

Some plants climb with **tendrils.**

Leaves, stems or flowers may bear sticky-feeling **glands,** sometimes at the ends of minute hairs.

Kinds of fruit:

achene — has one seed

follicle — one chamber, several seeds, splits on one side

capsule — has two or more several-seeded chambers

These symbols show the life zone where each species is most likely to grow.

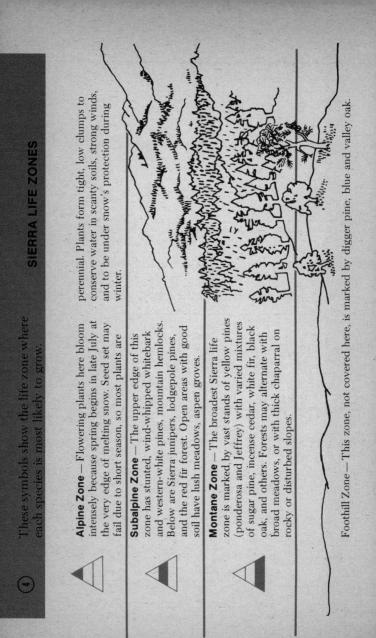

Alpine Zone — Flowering plants here bloom intensely because spring begins in late July at the very edge of melting snow. Seed set may fail due to short season, so most plants are perennial. Plants form tight, low clumps to conserve water in scanty soils, strong winds, and to be under snow's protection during winter.

Subalpine Zone — The upper edge of this zone has stunted, wind-whipped whitebark and western-white pines, mountain hemlocks. Below are Sierra junipers, lodgepole pines, and the red fir forest. Open areas with good soil have lush meadows, aspen groves.

Montane Zone — The broadest Sierra life zone is marked by vast stands of yellow pines (ponderosa and Jeffrey) with varied mixtures of sugar pine, incense cedar, white fir, black oak, and others. Forests may alternate with broad meadows, or with thick chaparral on rocky or disturbed slopes.

Foothill Zone — This zone, not covered here, is marked by digger pine, blue and valley oak.

East Slope — Winter and summer storms drop most of their moisture climbing up the west slope. Air descending into the Great Basin warms and dries as it goes. This zone harbors high-desert plants like mountain mahogany, sagebrush, pinyon, juniper, as well as the more drought-tolerant west-slope trees: Jeffrey pine, and (nearer the crest) lodgepole pine and white fir. Plants of this zone are indicated by an **E** next to the range symbol:

```
N
C E
S
```

Zone Altitudes — It's hard to give exact altitudes for life zones. Zones are at lower altitudes toward the north, higher in the south. Alpine plants, for instance, grow above 11,000 feet on Mount Whitney, at around 8,000 feet in the northern Sierra, and at sea level in the arctic. Zones will be higher on south-facing slopes warmed and dried by extra sun, and lower on cooler north-facing slopes. Basins collect heavy, cold night air, are chillier than adjacent slopes and ridges, and often in a colder life zone. If you want to know what life zone you're in, the kinds of trees present are often the best indicator.

Forest Shade — Plants here often have thin, broad leaves to absorb weak light. Some extract energy from associations with fungi in deep, decaying leaf mold. Plants are most luxuriant in brighter openings and along forest edges.

Rocky, Sandy Soil — Plants here tend to form cushions or sprawling mats, and may have thick, leathery, waxy or hairy, water-conserving leaves — adaptations to coarse soil that retains little water, and to full exposure to wind and sun.

Meadows — Fertile, well watered soil in sunny meadows supports the lushest summer wildflowers. Bee heaven. Species vary from wettest parts to driest. Low spots grade into wetter habitat below.

Streamsides, Swamps, Bogs, Seeps — Spots with superabundant water have soggy or submerged soil which limits oxygen supply to roots and may also become acidic, making nitrogen and other soil nutrients unavailable — conditions which often exclude all but specialized plants.

Disturbed areas — Bulldozers, wheels, trampling feet, fire and grazing make exposed, often compacted soils which are then invaded by alien or weed-like plants, some of which are familiar on farms or in cities.

Chaparral — Old burned areas slowly regenerate the forest, but first a woody-shrub stage appears. Wildflowers are limited to openings in this dense shrub cover.

BEGIN HERE

If the major leaf veins run parallel as in a blade of grass, go to → below

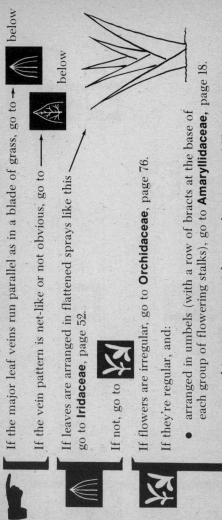

If the vein pattern is net-like or not obvious, go to ——→ below

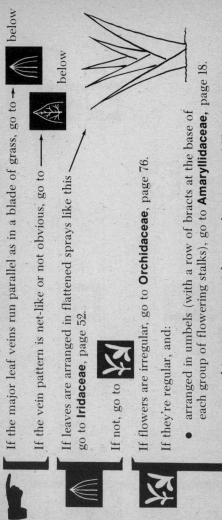

If leaves are arranged in flattened sprays like this go to **Iridaceae**, page 52.

If not, go to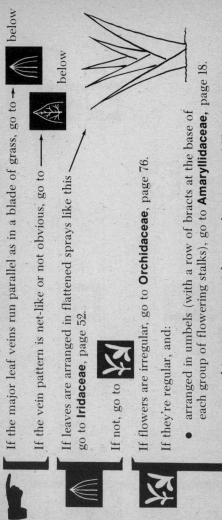

If flowers are irregular, go to **Orchidaceae**, page 76.

If they're regular, and:

• arranged in umbels (with a row of bracts at the base of each group of flowering stalks), go to **Amaryllidaceae**, page 18.

• arranged in racemes, panicles, or solitary, go to **Liliaceae**, page 63.

If many stemless small flowers are crowded together into what looks like a single flower, go to **Compositae**, page 26.

If not, go to ————————————→ next page

If flowers lack colored petals or sepals, go to **Ranunculaceae**, page 93.

If colored petals or sepals are present, and:

- all of them are separate, not joined, go to

- some or all of them are joined, at least at their bases, and flowers are:

  – regular, go to

  – irregular, go to ──────────────▶ page 16

If the number of petals (or colored sepals) on each flower is:

- three or six, go to ──────────────────────────────────▶ next page

- four, go to ──────▶ page 10

- five, go to ──────────────────────────────────▶ page 11

- indefinite, or if petals grade into sepals, go to ──────▶ page 9

If ovary is superior, go to ────▶ page 14

If it's inferior, go to ──────────────────────────────────▶ page 16

If plants grow in water and have arrowhead shaped leaves, go to **Alismaceae**, page 18.

If they have just three large leaves, go to **Liliaceae**, page 63.

If they're not as above, go to ————→

If the vein pattern on the leaves is net-like, go to ————→

If the vein pattern is hard to see, or if the main veins run parallel to each other, go to ————→

page 7

If there are:

- spines, go to **Papaveraceae**, page 78.

- long, spidery, maroon sepals, go to **Aristolochiaceae**, page 20.

- three-sided fruits containing a single seed, go to **Polygonaceae**, page 84.

If petals are red-maroon, go to **Paeoniaceae**, page 78.

If petals are yellow, plants grow in water with floating leaves, go to **Nymphaeaceae**, page 72.

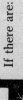

If many small flowers form a dense head like a single flower, go to **Compositae**, page 26.

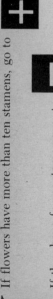

If flowers have more than ten stamens, go to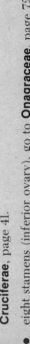

If they have fewer stamens, go to ▬

If sepals fall as flower opens, and there is one compound pistil, go to **Papaveraceae,** page 78.

If sepals stay on flower, and there are several separate pistils, go to **Ranunculaceae,** page 93.

If flowers are in dense, matted clusters, go to **Portulacaceae,** page 88.

If not, go to

If each flower has:

- four stamens (superior ovary, turned-back petals), go to **Primulaceae,** page 90.

- six stamens, four long, two short (superior ovary), go to **Cruciferae,** page 41.

- eight stamens (inferior ovary), go to **Onagraceae,** page 72.

- ten stamens (ovary superior to half-inferior), go to **Saxifragaceae,** page 103.

If plants have ordinary leaves, go to ⟶ next page

If they have unusual leaves which are:

- thick, fleshy, succulent, go to
- modified into insect traps, go to
- pale green, mottled, or without chlorophyll (on plants growing in deep leaf mold), go to **Pyrolaceae**, page 91.

If flowers have:

- two sepals, or if pistils are completely fused, go to **Portulacaceae**, page 88.
- five sepals, pistils only scarcely fused, go to **Crassulaceae**, page 40.

If leaves are:

- cobra-like with hood and fangs, go to **Sarraceniaceae**, page 102.
- spoon-shaped, covered with sticky hairs, go to **Droseraceae**, page 46.
- finely divided, bearing dark bladders under water, go to **Lentibulariaceae**, page 62.

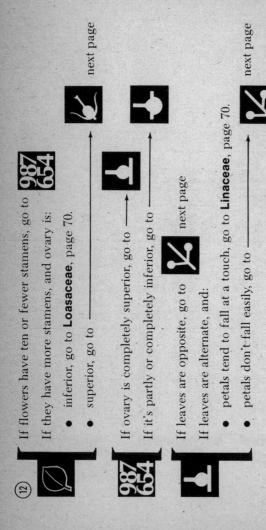

If flowers have ten or fewer stamens, go to 🄽🄾🄿

If they have more stamens, and ovary is:

- inferior, go to **Loasaceae**, page 70.
- superior, go to ——————————— next page

If ovary is completely superior, go to ———→

If it's partly or completely inferior, go to ———→ next page

If leaves are opposite, go to ———→

If leaves are alternate, and:

- petals tend to fall at a touch, go to **Linaceae**, page 70.
- petals don't fall easily, go to ———————— next page

If leaves are simple, go to **Saxifragaceae**, page 103.

If leaves are compound, and:

- over 0.6m long, go to **Araliaceae**, page 20.
- shorter, aromatic, go to **Umbelliferae**, page 115.

If there are two sepals, go to **Portulacaceae,** page 88.

If there are more sepals, go to **Caryophyllaceae,** page 24.

If styles lengthen into a beak-like structure as ovary ripens, and leaves have green stipules, go to **Geraniaceae,** page 48.

If style and stigma resemble an umbrella handle, go to **Pyrolaceae,** page 91.

If styles are not as above, and:

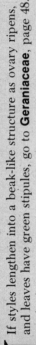

- leaves have papery stipules, go to **Polygonaceae,** page 84.

- leaves lack stipules, go to **Saxifragaceae,** page 103.

If stamens are fused together into a hollow tube, go to **Malvaceae,** page 71.

If not, go to ⟶

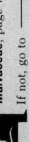

If leaves have:

- stipules at the base; floral bracts are present, go to **Rosaceae,** page 98.

- black dots (glands, use hand lens); stamens in bunches, go to **Hypericaceae,** page 52.

- neither of the above features, go to **Ranunculaceae,** page 93.

（14）

If plants are vines, go to **Convolvulaceae**, page 39.

If they're not vines, and:

- have milky sap, go to   next page

- are without milky sap, go to

If flowers are in coiled clusters, and stigma is:

- two-forked; fruit a many-seeded capsule, go to **Hydrophyllaceae**, page 49.

- undivided; fruit of four nutlets, go to **Boraginaceae**, page 22.

If flowers are not in coiled clusters, go to

If plants lack chlorophyll, go to **Pyrolaceae**, page 91.

If plants are green, and:

- stigma is three-lobed, or plants smell skunky, go to **Polemoniaceae**, page 79.

- stigma is otherwise, go to  next page

If flowers have hoods around center, go to **Asclepiadaceae**, page 21.

If flowers lack hoods, and leaves are:

- arrowhead-shaped, go to **Convolvulaceae**, page 39.
- some other shape, go to **Apocynaceae**, page 20.

If petals spread wide, go to —————→

If they converge into a bowl- or saucer-shaped corolla, and plants are:

- woody at base, go to **Ericaceae**, page 45.
- not woody, and leaves are:
  - basal, go to **Hydrophyllaceae**, page 49.
  - along stem, opposite, go to **Gentianaceae**, page 47.

If leaves are alternate, and flowers are:

- blue-purple, go to **Solanaceae**, page 114.
- yellow, go to **Scrophulariaceae**, page 106.

If leaves are opposite or whorled, and flowers are:

- pinkish to red, go to **Primulaceae**, page 90.
- greenish, white and fringed, or purple, go to **Gentianaceae**, page 47.

16

If leaves are opposite, and flowers are tightly clustered, go to **Valerianaceae**, page 119.

If leaves are opposite or whorled, but flowers are not tightly clustered, go to **Rubiaceae**, page 102.

If leaves are alternate, go to ⟶

If leaves are compound, go to  ⟶

If they're simple, go to **Campanulaceae**, page 23.

If leaves are over 0.6 m long, go to **Araliaceae**, page 20.

If they're shorter, go to **Umbelliferae**, page 115.

If all petals are fused to form a tube or sac, go to ⟶ next page

If only some petals are fused, and others are separate, go to

If the number of stamens is:

- four or six; leaves fern-like, go to **Fumariaceae**, page 46.
- ten; flowers pea-like, go to **Leguminosae**, page 57.
- more than ten, go to **Ranunculaceae**, page 93.

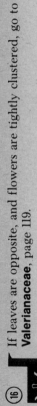

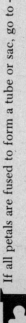

If ovary is inferior, go to **Valerianaceae**, page 119.

If ovary is superior, and:

- plant lacks chlorophyll, go to **Orobanchaceae**, page 77.
- plant lives in water; leaves submerged, go to **Lentibulariaceae**, page 62.
- plant is unlike the above, go to

If the top of the flower has two separate petals like this with lines marking the lower petal, go to **Violaceae**, page 120.

If a single petal or a fused pair of petals is centered at the top like this

or this ⟶

go to

If leaves have an odor when crushed; fruit is of four nutlets, go to **Labiatae**, page 54.

If leaves lack aroma; fruit a many-seeded capsule, go to **Scrophulariaceae**, page 106.

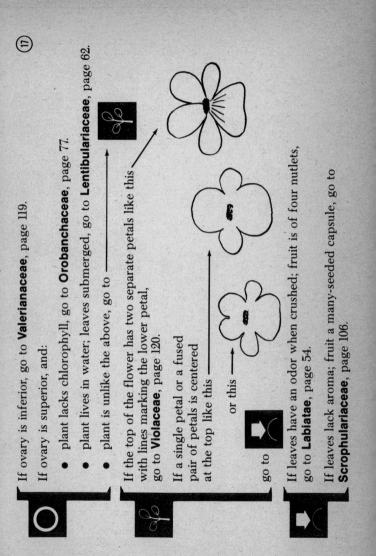

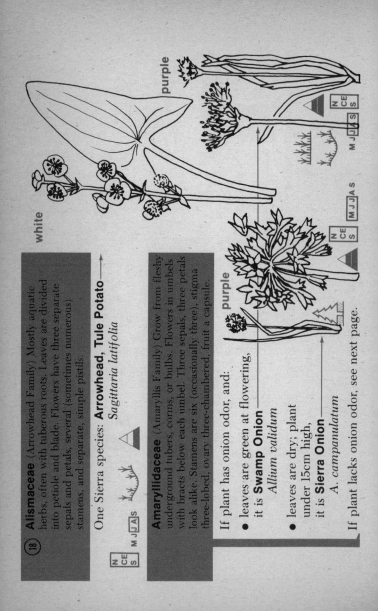

white

(18) **Alismaceae** (Arrowhead Family) Mostly aquatic herbs, often with tuberous roots. Leaves are divided into petiole and blade. Flowers have three separate sepals and petals, several (sometimes numerous) stamens, and separate, simple pistils.

One Sierra species: **Arrowhead, Tule Potato** →
Sagittaria latifolia

N
CE
S
M J J A S

purple

Amaryllidaceae (Amaryllis Family) Grow from fleshy underground tubers, corms, or bulbs. Flowers in umbels with bracts below each umbel. Three sepals, three petals look alike. Stamens are six (occasionally three), stigma three-lobed, ovary three-chambered, fruit a capsule.

If plant has onion odor, and:

• leaves are green at flowering,
  it is **Swamp Onion**
  Allium validum

• leaves are dry; plant
  under 15cm high,
  it is **Sierra Onion**,
  A. campanulatum

purple

N
CE
S
M J J A S

If plant lacks onion odor, see next page.

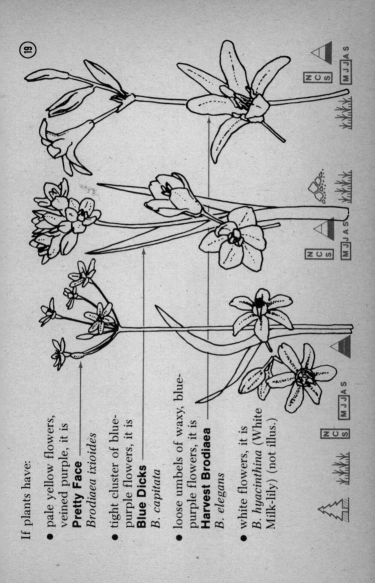

If plants have:

- pale yellow flowers, veined purple, it is **Pretty Face** *Brodiaea ixioides*

- tight cluster of blue-purple flowers, it is **Blue Dicks** *B. capitata*

- loose umbels of waxy, blue-purple flowers, **Harvest Brodiaea** *B. elegans*

- white flowers, it is *B. hyacinthina* (White Milk-lily) (not illus.)

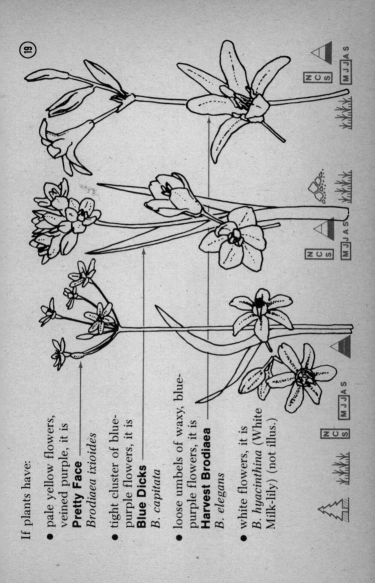

⑲

pink

green-white

maroon-brown

⑳ Apocynaceae (Dogbane Family). Paired, entire leaves with milky juice. Flowers with five sepals, five partly fused petals, five stamens. Two separate ovaries join above to a common style and stigma. Closely related to milkweeds, but lack hoods.

One Sierra species: **Common Dogbane**
Apocynum pumilum

Araliaceae (Aralia Family). Giant, compound leaves and compound umbels of flowers. Flower details like Parsley Family, except for berry type fruits.

One Sierra species: **Spikenard, Elk Clover**
Aralia californica

Aristolochiaceae (Pipevine Family) Creeping or viny plants with entire leaves. Flowers lack petals but have three partly -fused, oddly colored sepals. Reproductive parts hidden inside sepal cup. Fruit a capsule.

One Sierra species: **Sierra Wild Ginger**
Asarum hartwegii

Asclepiadaceae (Milkweed Family) Leaves are opposite or whorled, have milky juice. Flowers are in loose umbels, have five sepals and petals. Petals are augmented by five hoods (actually, outgrowths of stamen filaments). Two separate, one-chambered ovaries are joined on top by style and five-sided stigma. Stamens are complex, partly fused to side of stigma.

If leaves are:

● hairless, heart-shaped, blue-green, it is **Heart-leaved Milkweed**
  Asclepias cordifolia

● fuzzy, wooly, broad, it is **Showy Milkweed**
  A. speciosa

● narrow, whorled, it is **Whorled Milkweed**
  A. fascicularis

red-purple   purple   white

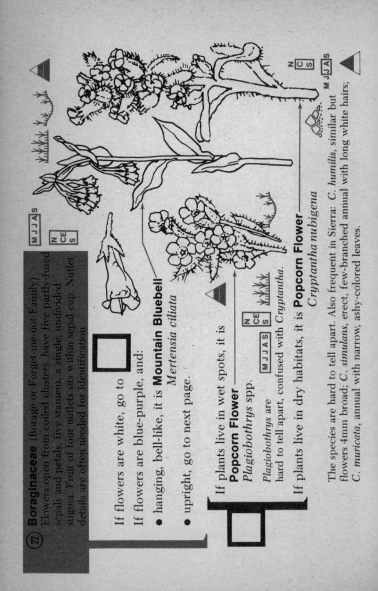

22 **Boraginaceae** (Borage or Forget-me-not Family)
Flowers open from coiled clusters, have five partly-fused sepals and petals, five stamens, a single, undivided stigma. Fruit of four nutlets sits within sepal cup. Nutlet details are often needed for identification.

If flowers are white, go to

If flowers are blue-purple, and:

• hanging, bell-like, it is **Mountain Bluebell**
  Mertensia ciliata

• upright, go to next page.

M J J A S
N
CE
s

If plants live in wet spots, it is
Popcorn Flower
Plagiobothrys spp.

Plagiobothrys are
hard to tell apart, confused with *Cryptantha*.

If plants live in dry habitats, it is **Popcorn Flower**
Cryptantha nubigena

N
CE
s

M J J A S

The species are hard to tell apart. Also frequent in Sierra: *C. humilis*, similar but flowers 4mm broad; *C. simulans*, erect, few-branched annual with long white hairs; *C. muricata*, annual with narrow, ashy-colored leaves.

N
C
s

M J J A s

If the nutlets have spreading segments
(look at older, wilted flowers), it is

Mountain Hound's Tongue
Cynoglossum occidentale

If fruit segments don't spread, it is

**Stickseed
Mountain Forget-me-not**
Hackelia jessicae

Less common stickseeds include: *H. nervosa,
H. longituba, H. velutina, H. californica, H. mundula.*

Campanulaceae (Bellflower Family) Mostly
herbs with simple leaves, milky juice. Flowers
often bell-shaped or tubular with five sepals,
petals, stamens; petals fused. Stigma three-lobed.
Ovary three-chambered. Fruit a capsule.

One Sierra species:

California Harebell
Campanula prenanthoides

blue

(24) **Caryophyllaceae** (Pink Family) Leaves paired (opposite), attached to swollen nodes of stem. Sepals mostly five, sometimes partly fused. Petals five but separate, often notched or fringed ("pinked"). Stamen and style number varies. Upper half of ovary has central, unattached stalk bearing many seeds in capsule that later splits.

If leaves are very narrow, almost needle-like; plants forming cushions, go to → 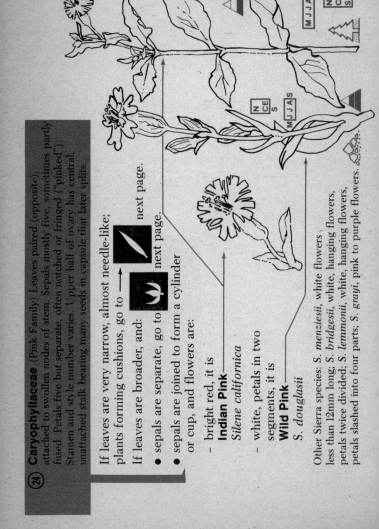 next page.

If leaves are broader, and:

● sepals are separate, go to 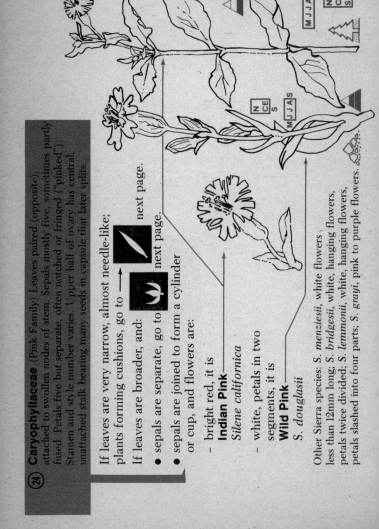 next page.

● sepals are joined to form a cylinder or cup, and flowers are:

– bright red, it is
 Indian Pink
 Silene californica

– white, petals in two segments, it is
 Wild Pink
 S. douglasii

Other Sierra species: *S. menziesii*, white flowers less than 12mm long; *S. bridgesii*, white, hanging flowers, petals twice divided; *S. lemmonii*, white, hanging flowers, petals slashed into four parts; *S. grayi*, pink to purple flowers.

white   white   (25)

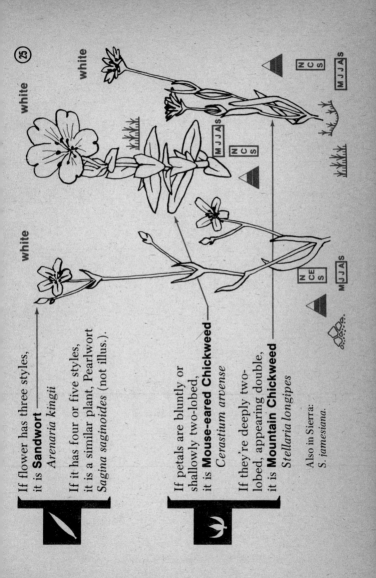

If flower has three styles,
it is **Sandwort**
   Arenaria kingii

If it has four or five styles,
it is a similar plant, Pearlwort
Sagina saginoides (not illus.).

If petals are bluntly or
shallowly two-lobed,
it is **Mouse-eared Chickweed**
   Cerastium arvense

If they're deeply two-
lobed, appearing double,
it is **Mountain Chickweed**
   Stellaria longipes

Also in Sierra:
S. jamesiana.

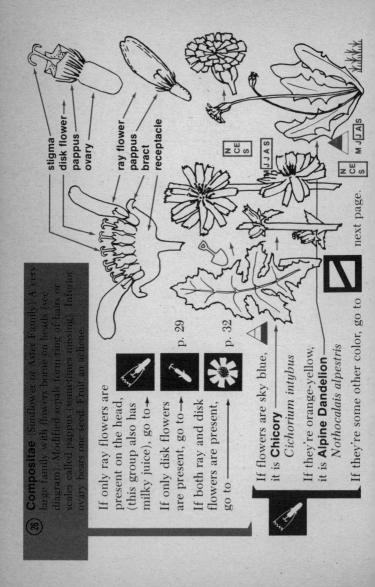

25 Compositae (Sunflower or Aster Family) A very large family with flowers borne on heads (see diagram). Modified sepals form ring of hairs or scales called pappus (sometimes missing). Inferior ovary bears one seed. Fruit an achene.

stigma
disk flower
pappus
ovary

ray flower
pappus
bract
receptacle

If only ray flowers are present on the head, (this group also has milky juice), go to → p. 29

If only disk flowers are present, go to →

If both ray and disk flowers are present, go to → p. 32

If flowers are sky blue, it is **Chicory**
Cichorium intybus

If they're orange-yellow, it is **Alpine Dandelion**
Nothocalais alpestris

If they're some other color, go to next page.

If pappus is attached to a narrow beak on top of ovary, go to ⟶

If pappus is attached directly to top of ovary, go to ⟶

If flower heads are borne singly on ends of non-leafy stems, it is
Common Dandelion
Taraxacum officinale

If flower heads are several on a leafy stem, it is
Hawksbeard
Crepis intermedia

Other hard-to-tell-apart hawksbeards include *C. nana,*
C. occidentalis, C. pleurocarpa, C. acuminata.

pinkish

If all leaves are basal, go to next page.

If some are on stem, it is
Stephanomeria

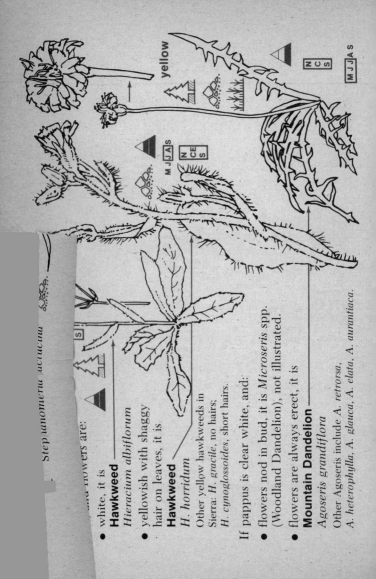

...a flowers are:

- white, it is
  Hawkweed
  Hieracium albiflorum

- yellowish with shaggy hair on leaves, it is
  Hawkweed
  H. horridum
  Other yellow hawkweeds in Sierra: *H. gracile*, no hairs; *H. cynoglossoides*, short hairs.

If pappus is clear white, and:

- flowers nod in bud, it is *Microseris* spp. (Woodland Dandelion), not illustrated.

- flowers are always erect, it is
  Mountain Dandelion
  Agoseris grandiflora
  Other Agoseris include *A. retrorsa*, *A. heterophylla*, *A. glauca*, *A. elata*, *A. aurantiaca*.

yellow

If flower heads have wooly hairs on the bracts, and individual flowers are hard to find, go to ⟶ **white to rose**

If heads have spiny bracts, go to next page.

If heads are not as above, go to ⟶

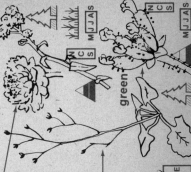

If plants grow as creeping mats; flowering stems less than 15cm high; both sides of leaf wooly, it is **Pink Pussy Toes** ⟶
Antennaria rosea
Less common are *A. dimorpha, A. alpina, A. argentea.*

If plants grow as clumps; flowering stems over 30cm high; leaves wooly underneath, it is **Pearly Everlasting**   **white**
Anaphalis margaritacea

If flowers are blue to purple, go to **B** p. 31

If they're yellow, go to ⟶ **Y** p. 31

If they're greenish or whitish, and:

• leaves are arrowhead-shaped, silvery beneath, it is **Trail Marker Plant**   **green**
Adenocaulon bicolor

• leaves are otherwise, it is
Pincushion Flower   **white**
Chaenactis douglasii
Less common are *C. alpigena* (forms woody-based mats), and *C. nevadensis.*

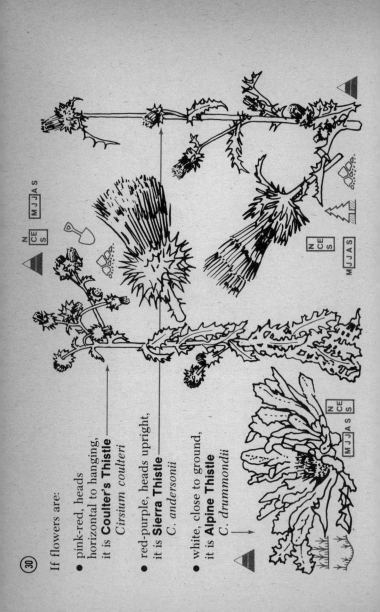

30

If flowers are:

- pink-red, heads
  horizontal to hanging,
  it is **Coulter's Thistle**
  Cirsium coulteri

- red-purple, heads upright,
  it is **Sierra Thistle**
  C. andersonii

- white, close to ground,
  it is **Alpine Thistle**
  C. drummondii

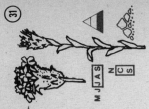

B

If outer disk flowers are larger than middle ones; leaves alternate, it is **Purple Pincushions** *Lessingia leptoclada*

If outer flowers are not larger; leaves are paired, it is **Western Thoroughwort** *Eupatorium occidentale*

Y

If leaves are deeply divided, or if they are alternate, go to ➤

If they're neither deeply divided nor alternate, but are:

• paired along stems, see Arnica, p. 32.

• mostly at base, see Raillardella, p. 32.

If bracts around flower heads are green at tips, and:

• leaves end in abrupt points (miniature spines), it is **Rayless Golden Aster** *Chrysopsis breweri*

• leaf tips are smooth, it is a rayless Aster. See p. 34.

If bracts on flower heads are some other color at their tips, it is a rayless variety of Fleabane. See Fleabane, p. 34.

yellow

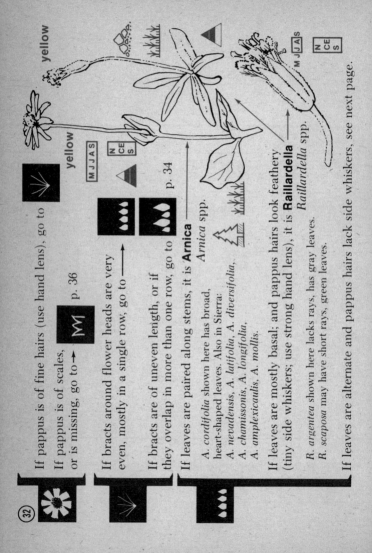

yellow

If pappus is of fine hairs (use hand lens), go to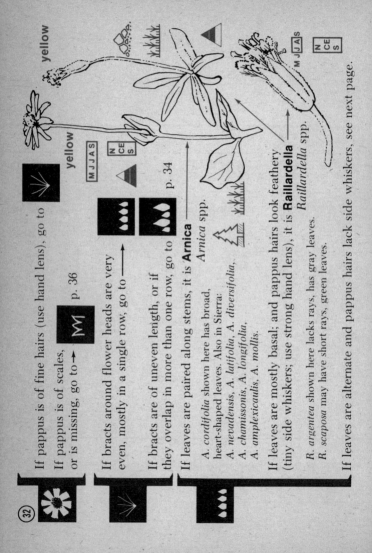

If pappus is of scales, or is missing, go to → p. 36

yellow

If bracts around flower heads are very even, mostly in a single row, go to →

If bracts are of uneven length, or if they overlap in more than one row, go to p. 34

If leaves are paired along stems, it is **Arnica** *Arnica* spp.

A. *cordifolia* shown here has broad, heart-shaped leaves. Also in Sierra: A. *nevadensis*, A. *latifolia*, A. *diversifolia*, A. *chamissonis*, A. *longifolia*, A. *amplexicaulis*, A. *mollis*.

If leaves are mostly basal; and pappus hairs look feathery (tiny side whiskers; use strong hand lens), it is **Raillardella** *Raillardella* spp.

R. *argentea* shown here lacks rays, has gray leaves. R. *scaposa* may have short rays, green leaves.

If leaves are alternate and pappus hairs lack side whiskers, see next page.

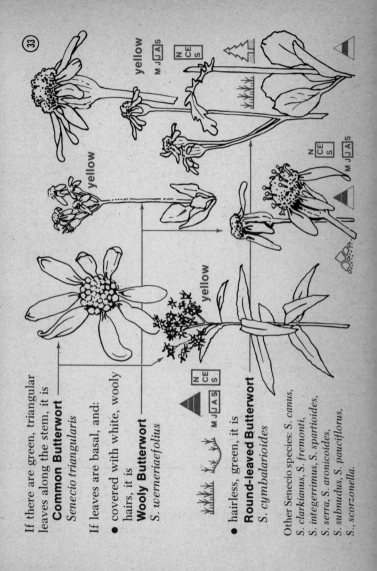

If there are green, triangular leaves along the stem, it is
Common Butterwort
Senecio triangularis

If leaves are basal, and:

● covered with white, wooly hairs, it is
Wooly Butterwort
S. werneriaefolius

● hairless, green, it is
Round-leaved Butterwort
S. cymbalarioides

Other Senecio species: *S. canus,*
S. clarkianus, S. fremonti,
S. integerrimus, S. spartioides,
S. serra, S. aronicoides,
S. subnudus, S. pauciflorus,
S., scorzonella.

yellow

yellow

yellow

yellow

N CE S
M J A S

N CE S
M J A S

N CE S
M J A S

If ray flowers are bright yellow, go to next page.

If they're white, blue or purple, go to

variable color

If bracts around flower heads are green at their tips, it is **Aster**
Aster spp.

A. foliaceus (Leafy Aster) shown here is typical of the many species in Sierra which are hard to tell apart: *A. occidentalis, A. adscendens, A. radulinus, A. alpigenus, A. oregonensis, A. integrifolius, A. campestris.*

If tips of bracts are not green, it is

Fleabane
Wild Daisy
Erigeron spp.

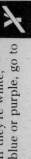

E. coulteri shown here is typical of many similar species in Sierra: *E. peregrinus, E. vagus, E. lonchophyllus, E. breweri, E. compositus, E. pygmaeus, E. divergens, E. miser, E. petiolaris, E. inornatus.*

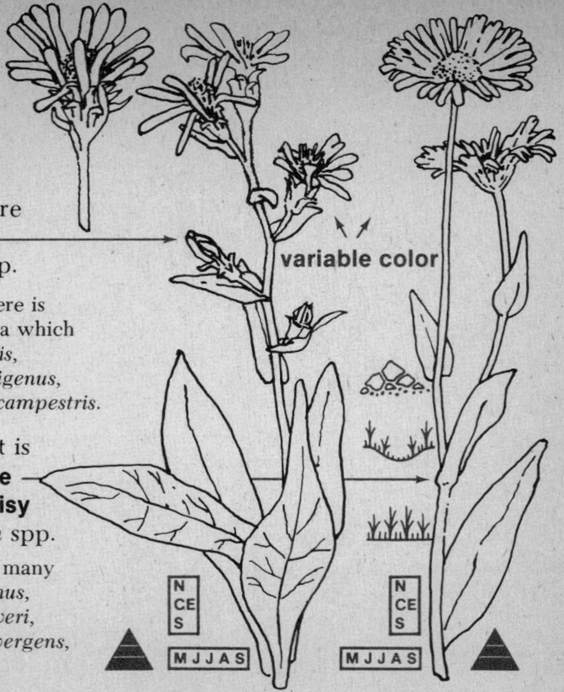

If flower heads are pea-sized or smaller, in spike-like clusters, it is

Goldenrod

Solidago spp.

S. *elongata* shown here has hairless leaves, toothed, mostly clustered at plant base.
S. *californica* is similar, but leaves lack teeth, have small hairs. S. *multiradiata* has well developed leaves up the stems.

N CE S   M J A S

If flower heads are larger, fewer per cluster; and leaves:

● have conspicuous white hairs, it is **Golden Aster**
  Chrysopsis villosa

● are not conspicuously hairy (look green), it is **Bush Sunflower**
  Haplopappus spp.

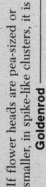

H. *acaulis* shown here has densely crowded leaves hiding basal, woody stems.
H. *apargioides* lacks wood, grows from taproot. H. *suffruticosus* makes low, mounded, woody subshrubs with narrow leaves.

N CE S   M J A S

If ray flowers are yellow, go to

If they're white; foliage ferny, aromatic, it is **Yarrow**

Achillea lanulosa

If leaves and bracts have sticky glands, it is **Tarweed**

Madia spp.

M. *elegans* shown here has showy rays often marked at base with purple. Other common tarweeds are often smaller-flowered, including: *M. bolanderi, M. yosemitana, M. gracilis, M. glomerata, M. minima.*

If disk flowers are borne on a cone-shaped receptacle, it is **Coneflower**

Rudbeckia spp.

R. *californica* shown here has "cones" over 5cm long. R. *hirta* and R. *occidentalis* have less conspicuous cones.

If leaves and flowers are not as above, go to next page.

yellow

If there are papery scales *between* disk flowers *inside* the head, **yellow** go to

M J J A S

If not, go to next page

If stems are over 0.5m tall, and leafy, it is **California Sunflower** ⟶ *Helianthus californica*

N
C
S

M J J A S

If stems are shorter; leaves mostly at base, and:

- flowers have no páppus, it is **Balsamroot** *Balsamorhiza deltoidea*

B. sagittata may also be found in Sierra.

N
C
S

M J J A S

- flowers have scaly páppus, it is **Mule's Ear** *Wyethia mollis*

W. helenioides is sometimes found at lower elevations.

yellow!

If bracts around flower heads are in one row, it is **Wooly Sunflower**
Eriophyllum lanatum

If bracts are in more than one row or level, and:

- receptacle is rounded, rays turned down, it is
Sneezeweed
Helenium spp.

H. hoopesii shown here has conspicuous rays. *H. bigelovii* has smaller, not obvious rays.

- receptacle is flat, rays spreading, and rays are:

  - yellow, it is
  Mountain Sunflower
  Hulsea algida

  - purple, it is
  Purple Mountain Sunflower
  H. heterochroma (illustrated next page)

yellow

yellow

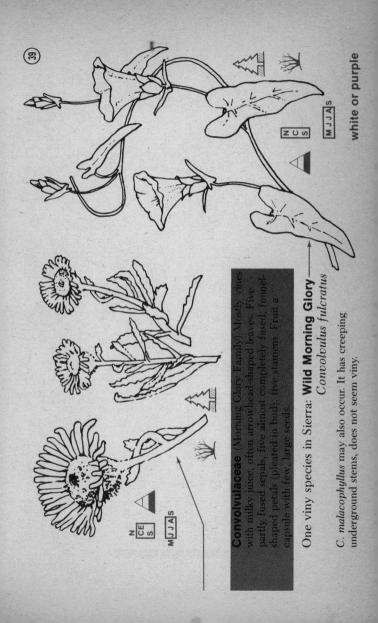

Convolvulaceae (Morning Glory Family) Mostly vines with milky juice, often arrowhead-shaped leaves. Five partly fused sepals, five almost completely fused funnel-shaped petals (pleated in bud), five stamens. Fruit a capsule with few, large seeds.

One viny species in Sierra: **Wild Morning Glory**
Convolvulus fulcratus

C. malacophyllus may also occur. It has creeping underground stems, does not seem viny.

white or purple

40 **Crassulaceae** (Live-forever or Orpine Family) Leaves very fleshy (succulent), flowers star-like with five free petals, five or ten stamens, several pistils with ovaries barely fused at bases.

If leaves are very narrow; flowers bright yellow, it is
Alpine Stonecrop
Sedum lanceolatum

If leaves are heart-shaped; flowers pale yellow, it is
Broad-leaved Stonecrop
S. obtusatum

If stems and flowers are red, it is
Rosecrown
S. rosea

Other species of this family in Sierra include *S. spathulifolium* (Common Stonecrop) with spoon-shaped leaves, bright yellow flowers; and less common species: *Dudleya cymosa*, tight rosettes of broad, pointed leaves; and *Parvisedum* spp., low annuals with leaves drying up.

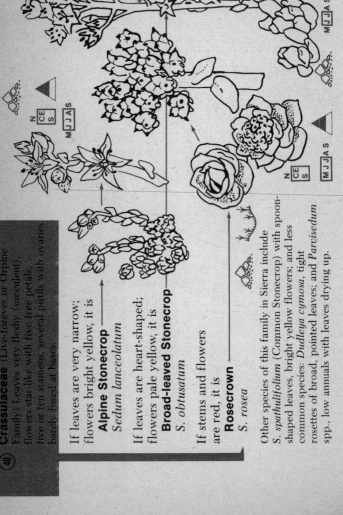

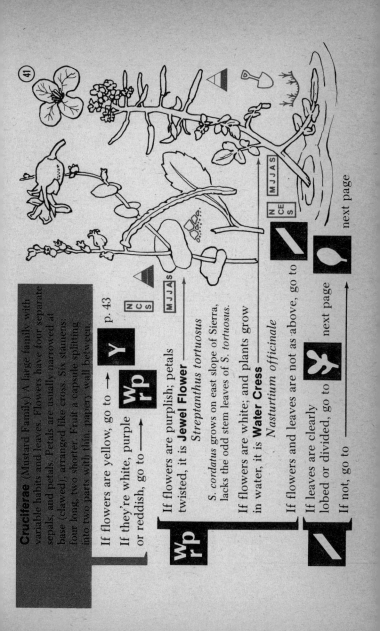

(41)

Cruciferae (Mustard Family) A large family with variable habits and leaves. Flowers have four separate sepals, and petals. Petals are usually narrowed at base (clawed), arranged like cross. Six stamens: four long, two shorter. Fruit a capsule splitting into two parts with thin, papery wall between

If flowers are yellow, go to → **Y** p. 43

If they're white, purple or reddish, go to → **Wp rp**

If flowers are purplish; petals twisted, it is **Jewel Flower**
Streptanthus tortuosus

S. *cordatus* grows on east slope of Sierra, lacks the odd stem leaves of S. *tortuosus*.

If flowers are white, and plants grow in water, it is **Water Cress**
Nasturtium officinale

If flowers and leaves are not as above, go to

If leaves are clearly lobed or divided, go to → next page

If not, go to → next page

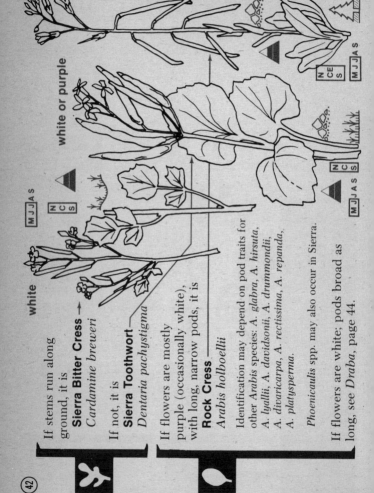

white

white or purple

If stems run along
ground, it is
Sierra Bitter Cress →
Cardamine breweri

If not, it is
Sierra Toothwort
Dentaria pachystigma

If flowers are mostly
purple (occasionally white),
with long, narrow pods, it is
Rock Cress
Arabis holboellii

Identification may depend on pod traits for
other *Arabis* species: *A. glabra, A. hirsuta,
A. lyallii, A. davidsonii, A. drummondii,
A. divaricarpa, A. rectissima, A. repanda,
A. platysperma.*

Phoenicaulis spp. may also occur in Sierra.

If flowers are white; pods broad as
long, see *Draba,* page 44.

42

Y

If leaves are simple (sometimes toothed, but unlobed), go to next page.

If they're divided like a fern, it is

Tansy Mustard
Descurainia richardsonii

D. californica may also occur in Sierra.

If they're deeply divided, but not fern-like; and plants grow in wet places, go to

If leaves have larger lobes at the tips; and pods are four-sided, it is **Winter Cress**
Barbarea orthoceras

If leaves are more evenly divided; pods cylindrical, it is **Yellow Cress** →
Rorippa curvisiliqua

If flowers are in spike-like racemes; and pods are long and narrow, it is
Sierra Wallflower
Erysimum perenne

If flowers are in small clusters or single; plants are low; and pods are broad, rounded, and:

● flat, it is
Whitlow Grass
Draba lemmonii

Other species include:
D. stenoloba, annual; *D. douglasii*, leathery leaves, white flowers; and *D. paysonii*, densely overlapping leaves, pale yellow flowers.

● inflated, it is
Bladderpod
Lesquerella occidentalis

Ericaceae (Heather Family) Usually woody plants. Leaves simple, entire, firm. Flowers have five sepals, five partly fused petals often forming urn shape. Stamens mostly ten, opening by special pores in their ends.

pink

If leaves are needle-like, go to ◣

If they're broader; plants prostrate, it is
Bog Laurel
Kalmia polifolia

If flowers are reddish, upright, it is
Red Heather
Phyllodoce breweri

If they're white, hanging, it is
White Heather
Cassiope mertensiana

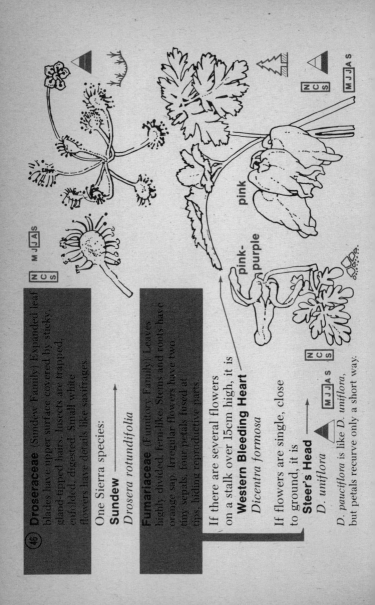

46 Droseraceae (Sundew Family) Expanded leaf blades have upper surface covered by sticky, gland-tipped hairs. Insects are trapped, enfolded, digested. Small white flowers have details like saxifrages.

One Sierra species:

Sundew ——▶
Drosera rotundifolia

Fumariaceae (Fumitory Family) Leaves highly divided, fern-like. Stems and roots have orange sap. Irregular flowers have two tiny sepals, four petals fused at tips, hiding reproductive parts.

If there are several flowers on a stalk over 15cm high, it is
Western Bleeding Heart
Dicentra formosa

If flowers are single, close to ground, it is
Steer's Head ——▶
D. uniflora

D. pauciflora is like *D. uniflora*, but petals recurve only a short way.

pink

pink-purple

Gentianaceae (Gentian Family) Plants mostly of mountain meadows. Leaves usually opposite. Flowers often cup-shaped with four or five sepals and petals partly fused, four or five stamens, many also have special appendages, glands, or pleats on petal. Ovary incomplete, two-chambered. Fruit a capsule

If leaves are divided into three parts; plants growing in water, it is
Buckbean, Bogbean
Menyanthes trifoliata

If leaves are
simple, go to

If flowers are cup-
or vase-shaped and:

• white, dotted with green;
stems short, it is **Alpine Gentian**
Gentiana newberryi

• blue, long, it is **Sierra Gentian**
G. holopetala

Less common in Sierra are: *G. calycosa*,
tall perennial, blue flowers; and *G. amarella*,
short, annual, petals shorter than 25mm.

If flowers are widely open, star-like, go to next page.

48 green & purple

If sepals, petals, stamens are five, it is

Swertia
Swertia perennis

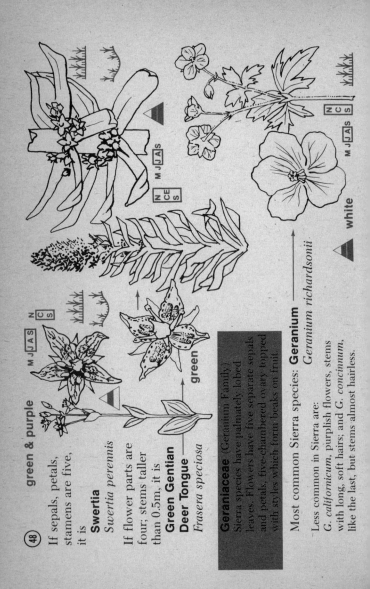

N
C
S

M J A S

If flower parts are four; stems taller than 0.5m, it is

Green Gentian
Deer Tongue —— green
Frasera speciosa

green & purple

N
CE
S

M J A S

white

M J A S

N
C
S

Geraniaceae (Geranium Family)
Sierra species have palmately lobed leaves. Flowers have five separate sepals and petals, five-chambered ovary topped with styles which form beaks on fruit.

Most common Sierra species: **Geranium**
Geranium richardsonii

Less common in Sierra are:
G. californicum, purplish flowers, stems with long, soft hairs; and *G. concinnum*, like the last, but stems almost hairless.

Hydrophyllaceae (Waterleaf Family) Leaves variable. Flowers, usually in coiled clusters (unrolling as buds open), have five partly fused petals, sepals, five stamens, two-parted stigma. Fruit a capsule with many seeds.

If leaves are lobed or compound, go to →

If they're mostly entire,
not deeply lobed, go to ——————→

If leaves are all at base of plant;
flowers white, it is **Meadow Beauty**
Similar is *H.*   *Hesperochiron californicus*
pumilis.

If leaves are paired on stems,
stems trailing, it is **Draperia**
                                      Draperia systyla

If leaves are alternate on stems; or,
if paired, stems are upright, go to next page.

If leaves are pinnately divided into narrow,
spoon-shaped segments, it is **Five Spot**
                                      Nemophila maculata

N. spatulata, with smaller, pure-white
flowers, is also found in Sierra.
If not, go to next page.   **purple**

white, purple spots

bluish

dull purple

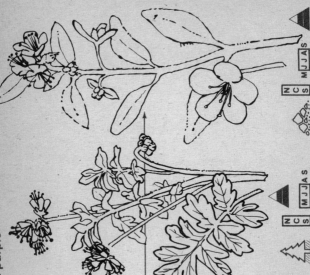

If leaves are clustered
near base of plant, it is
Waterleaf
Hydrophyllum occidentale

If leaves are distributed
along stems, go to ——→

If leaves
are undivided, it is
Phacelia
Phacelia racemosa

If they're twice divided
(divisions have divisions),
go to next page

If they're once divided,
go to next page

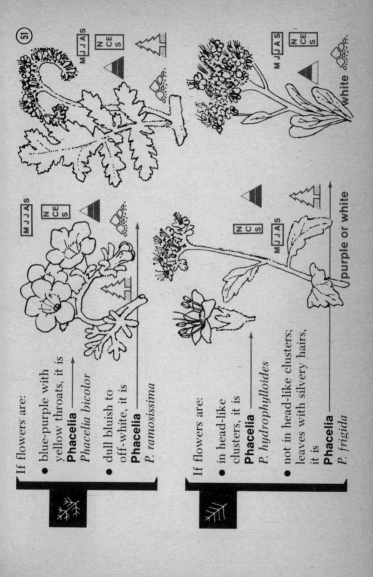

If flowers are:

- blue-purple with yellow throats, it is
  Phacelia
  Phacelia bicolor

- dull bluish to off-white, it is
  Phacelia
  P. ramosissima

MJJAs N CE s

If flowers are:

- in head-like clusters, it is
  Phacelia
  P. hydrophylloides

- not in head-like clusters; leaves with silvery hairs, it is
  Phacelia
  P. frigida

purple or white

white

MJJAs N CE s

M JJAs N C s

52 **Hypericaceae** (St Johnswort Family)
Entire, opposite leaves, with tiny black glands.
Flowers have five free sepals and petals,
numerous stamens clustered in bunches,
and compound pistil. Fruit a capsule.

If flowers are salmon-yellow,
tiny; plant grows close to
ground, it is
Tinker's Penny
Hypericum anagalloides

If flowers are bright
yellow, conspicuous;
plant upright, it is
St Johnswort
H. formosum

Iridaceae (Iris Family) Sword-like leaves are
arranged in flattened sprays so that bases overlap.
Flowers have three colored sepals and petals
and three stamens, styles and stigmas. Ovary
is inferior, three-chambered. Fruit a capsule

(Iris family is on next page.)

If there are conspicuous, drooping sepals and upright petals; and flowers are:

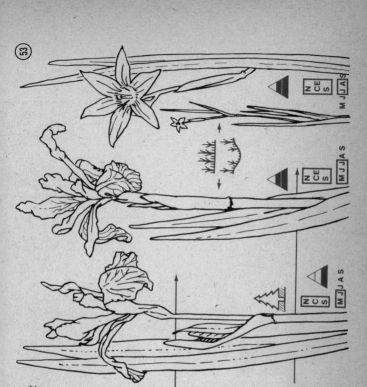

- pale yellow to purple, growing in pine forest, it is **Sierra Iris** **Rainbow Iris**
  Iris hartwegii

- blue-violet, growing in high meadow, it is **Meadow Iris**
  Iris missouriensis

If petals and sepals look alike; flowers are blue-purple with yellow centers, it is **Mountain Blue-eyed Grass**
Sisyrinchium idahoense

Similar, but with yellow flowers is *S. elmeri* (Yellow-eyed Grass).

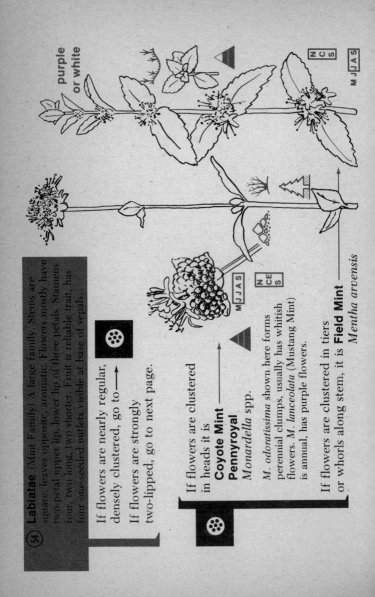

54 **Labiatae** (Mint Family) A large family. Stems are square, leaves opposite, aromatic. Flowers mostly have two-petal upper lip, lower lip of three petals. Stamens four, two long, two shorter. Fruit is reliable trait, has four one-seeded nutlets visible at base of sepals.

If flowers are nearly regular, densely clustered, go to ⟶

If flowers are strongly two-lipped, go to next page.

If flowers are clustered in heads it is
Coyote Mint
Pennyroyal
Monardella spp.

M. odoratissima shown here forms perennial clumps, usually has whitish flowers. *M. lanceolata* (Mustang Mint) is annual, has purple flowers.

If flowers are clustered in tiers or whorls along stem, it is **Field Mint**
Mentha arvensis

purple or white

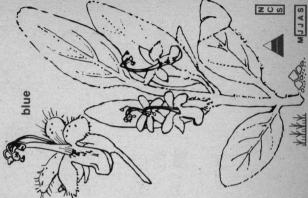

blue

white

If flowers are whorled, arranged in spikes, go to next page.

If flowers are in small groups, and:

- flowers look like Snapdragons, it is **Skullcap** →
  Scutellaria californica

- foliage is strong-smelling; stamens curled, it is **Blue Curls**
  Trichostema oblongum

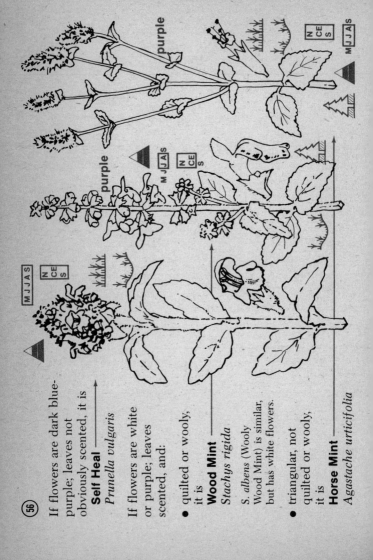

(56)

If flowers are dark blue-purple; leaves not obviously scented, it is

Self Heal
Prunella vulgaris

If flowers are white or purple; leaves scented, and:

- quilted or wooly, it is
Wood Mint
Stachys rigida

S. albens (Wooly Wood Mint) is similar, but has white flowers.

- triangular, not quilted or wooly, it is
Horse Mint
Agastache urticifolia

Leguminosae (Pea or Legume Family) An important family. Leaves have stipules at base, are most often pinnately compound, but in some groups are palmately compound or three-parted. Flowers have typical pea shape: back petal is called banner; two side petals, wings; two central, partly fused petals, the keel. Ten stamens are usually partly fused. Ovary forms single-chambered pod splitting lengthwise along two sides.

If leaves have just three leaflets, go to ──►

If there are more leaflets, and leaves are:

• pinnately compound, go to page 60.

• palmately compound, go to next page.

If flowers are in spikes, and are:

• white, it is **White Sweet Clover**
  Melilotus albus

• blue-purple,
  it is **Alfalfa**
  Medicago sativa

If flowers are in tight heads, at
least not in spikes, it is **Clover**
  Trifolium spp.

T. monanthum (Mountain Clover) shown here is common in high meadows, has few, white flowers per stem.

variable color

M J J A S
N
CE
S

M J J A S
N
CE
S

M J J A S
N
CE
S

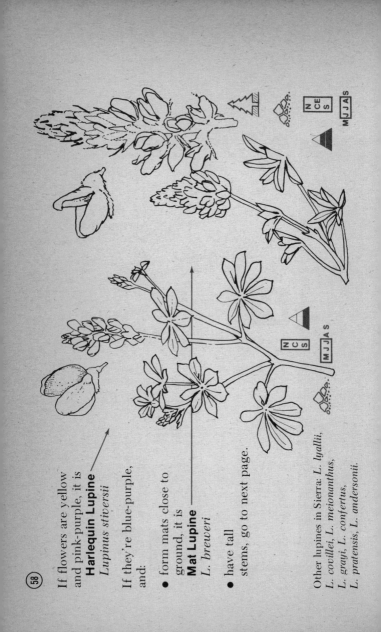

If flowers are yellow
and pink-purple, it is
Harlequin Lupine
Lupinus stiversii

If they're blue-purple,
and:

• form mats close to
  ground, it is
  Mat Lupine
  L. breweri

• have tall
  stems, go to next page.

Other lupines in Sierra: *L. lyallii,*
L. covillei, L. meionanthus,
L. grayi, L. confertus,
L. pratensis, L. andersonii.

(58)

If leaves have sparse, stiff hairs on top, it is
White-stemmed Lupine
Lupinus albicaulis

If leaves are hairless above; and main stems are:

● hollow, it is
Meadow Lupine
L. polyphyllus

● solid; leaves often wither at flowering, it is
Woodland Lupine
L. latifolius

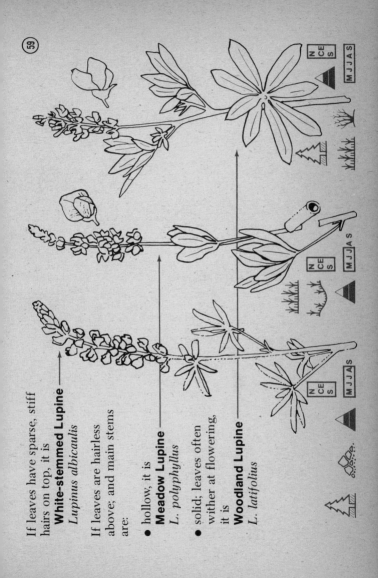

If plants are viny, and:

- wings of flower cling to keel part way along, it is **Vetch** ⟶ *Vicia* spp.

V. californica shown here is native. Many introduced vetches are roadside weeds.

MJJAs   purple   MJJAS

- wings are unattached to keel, and there are:

  – large, showy, pink to purplish flowers, winged stems, it is **Roadside Sweet Pea** ⟶ *Lathyrus latifolius*

  – clusters of small flowers which fade to striking sulfur-yellow-brown, it is **Sulfur Pea** ⟶ *L. sulphureus*

L. nevadensis (Mountain Sweet Pea), with small clusters of small purple and white flowers; and *L. pauciflorus* may also occur in Sierra.

If plants stand erect, without tendrils, go to next page.

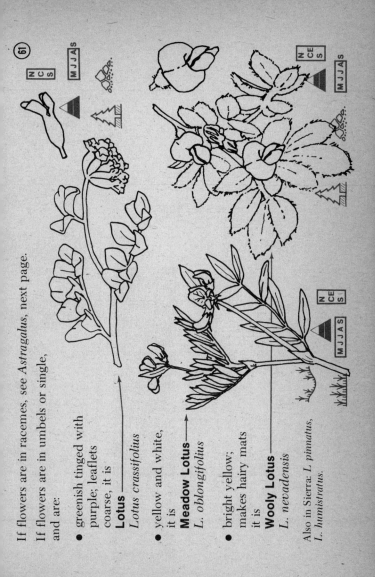

If flowers are in racemes, see *Astragalus*, next page.

If flowers are in umbels or single, and are:

● greenish tinged with
  purple; leaflets
  coarse, it is
  Lotus
  Lotus crassifolius

● yellow and white,
  it is
  Meadow Lotus
  L. oblongifolius

● bright yellow;
  makes hairy mats
  it is
  Wooly Lotus
  L. nevadensis

Also in Sierra: *L. pinnatus,*
  L. humistratus.

If pods have white hairs,
it is **Wooly Rattlepod**
Astragalus purshii

If they're spotted,
it is **Speckled Rattlepod**
A. whitneyi

Other rattlepods include:
A. bolanderi, A. lentiginosus,
A. austinae.

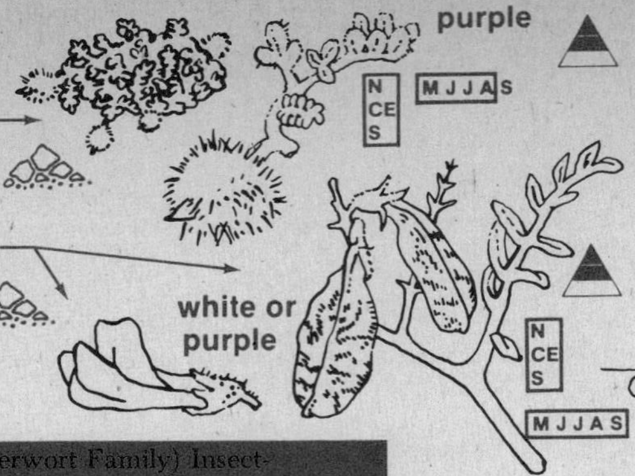
purple
N CE S
M J J A S
white or purple
N CE S
M J J A S

Lentibulariaceae (Bladderwort Family) Insect-catching plants in acidic lakes. Submerged, multibranched stems bear hair-like leaves and bladders which trap water animals. Only snapdragon-like flowers appear above water. Closely related to figworts.

One Sierra species: **Bladderwort**
Utricularia vulgaris

N C S
M J J A S

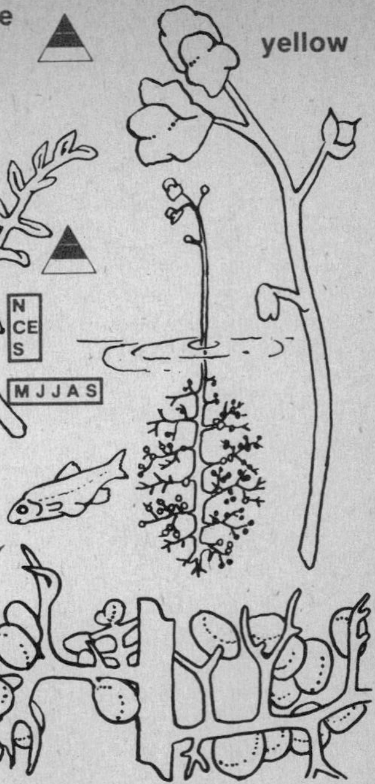
yellow

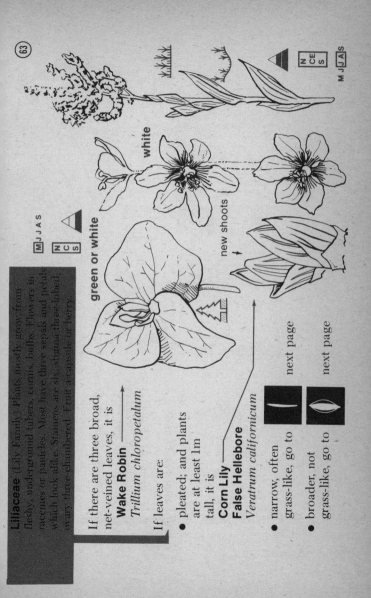

Liliaceae (Lily Family) Plants mostly grow from fleshy underground tubers, corms, bulbs. Flowers in racemes or panicles. Most have three sepals and petals which look alike. Stamens are six, stigma three-lobed, ovary three-chambered. Fruit a capsule or berry.

If there are three broad, net-veined leaves, it is
Wake Robin →
Trillium chloropetalum

If leaves are:

• pleated; and plants are at least 1m tall, it is
Corn Lily
False Hellebore →
Veratrum californicum

• narrow, often grass-like, go to   next page

• broader, not grass-like, go to   next page

green or white

white

new shoots

white

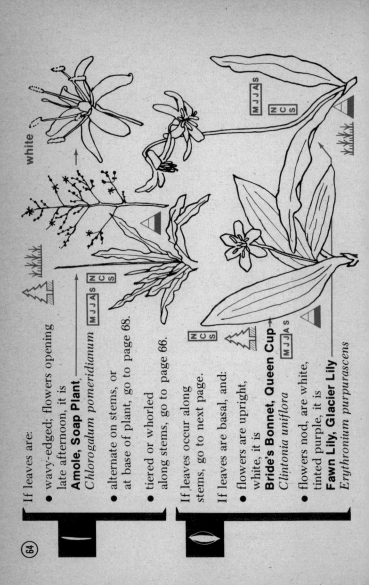

If leaves are:

- wavy-edged; flowers opening
  late afternoon, it is
  Amole, Soap Plant,
  Chlorogalum pomeridianum | M J J A S | N C S |

- alternate on stems, or
  at base of plant, go to page 68.

- tiered or whorled
  along stems, go to page 66.

If leaves occur along
stems, go to next page.

If leaves are basal, and:

- flowers are upright,
  white, it is
  Bride's Bonnet, Queen Cup→
  Clintonia uniflora | M J J A S | N C S |

- flowers nod, are white,
  tinted purple, it is
  Fawn Lily, Glacier Lily,
  Erythronium purpurascens | M J J A S | N C S |

64

If flowers hang under leaves, it is **Fairy Bells**
Disporum hookeri

white-green

If they're clustered beyond
leaves, and grow in:

● racemes, it is
Slim False Solomon's Seal
S. stellata

● dense panicles, it is
Fat False Solomon's Seal
Smilacina racemosa

white

white

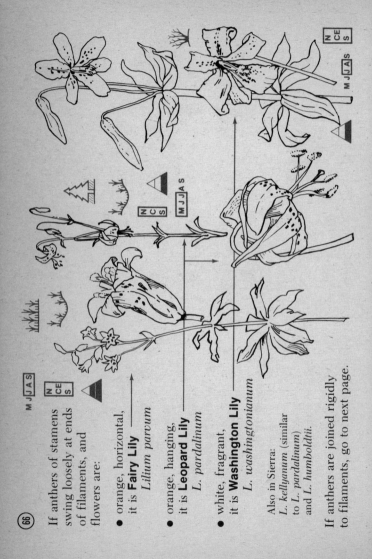

If anthers of stamens
swing loosely at ends
of filaments, and
flowers are:

- orange, horizontal,
  it is **Fairy Lily**
  Lilium parvum

- orange, hanging,
  it is **Leopard Lily**
  L. pardalinum

- white, fragrant,
  it is **Washington Lily**
  L. washingtonianum

Also in Sierra:
L. kellyanum (similar
to _L. pardalinum_)
and _L. humboldtii._

If anthers are joined rigidly
to filaments, go to next page.

If flowers are orange-red,
it is **Scarlet Fritillary** →
Fritillaria recurva

If they're brownish-
purple, checkered,
it is **Alpine Checker Lily**
F. atropurpurea

Other Sierra species include:
F. pinetorum (Pine Fritillary),
like *F. atropurpurea*; and
F. micrantha, with small brownish
or greenish, hanging flowers.

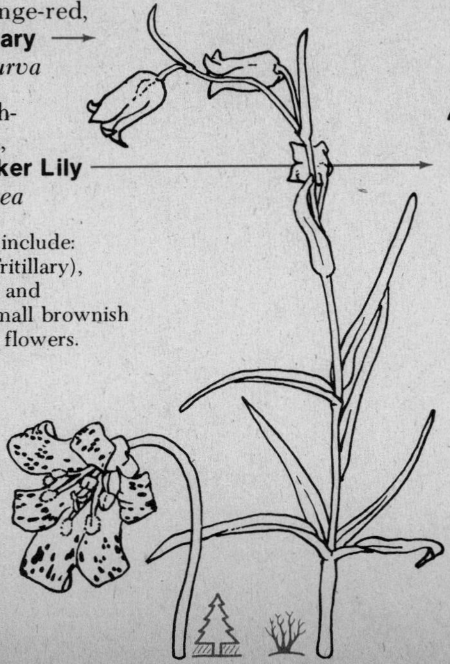

N
C
S

M J J A S

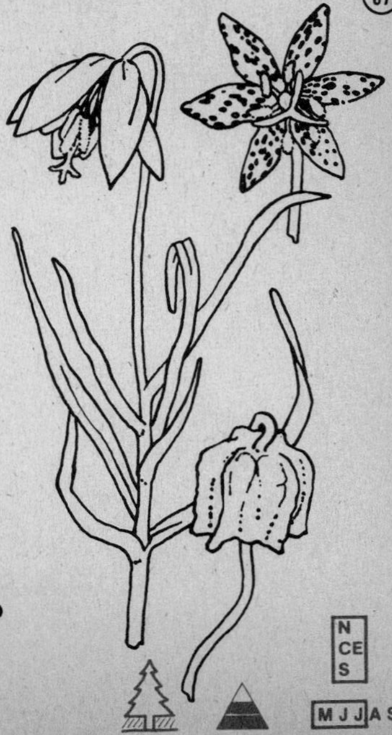

N
CE
S

M J J A S

If sepals and petals
look alike, go to next page.

If they look different from
each other, and flowers are:

- cup-shaped, white with
  dark brown and yellow
  spots inside, it is
  Sierra Mariposa Tulip
  Calochortus leichtlinii

- shallow, bowl-shaped,
  light purple, covered with
  purplish hairs, it is
  Purple Star Tulip
  C.coeruleus

Two small, white Star Tulips
occur in high meadows: *C. minimus*,
and *C. nudus*.

If flowers are white; petals have obvious glands, it is
Death Camass
Zygadenus venenosus

If flowers are blue, without glands, it is
Camass
Camassia leichtlinii

C. quamash, with less symmetrical petals also occurs in Sierra.

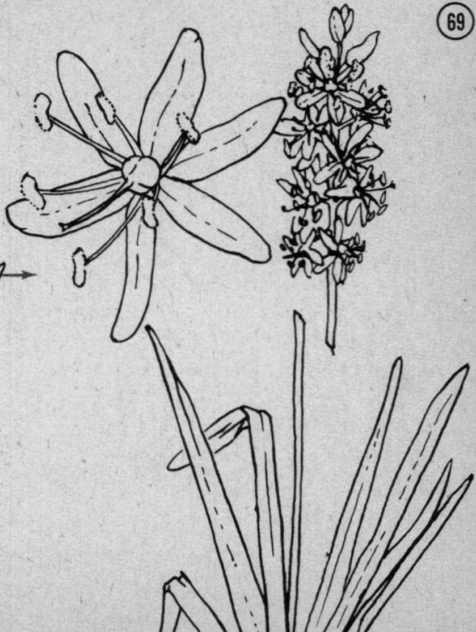

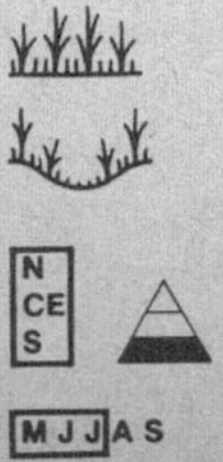

blue

yellow

(70) **Linaceae** (Flax Family) Flowers have five separate sepals and petals, five stamens. Petals fall at the slightest touch. Five styles on five-chambered ovary. Fruit a capsule.

Most common Sierra species:

Blue Flax
Linum lewisii

L. digynum also occurs.

Loasaceae (Blazing Star Family) Leaves feel sandpapery. Flowers have five sepals and petals, numerous stamens in bunches, inferior ovary. Fruit a many-seeded capsule.

One Sierra species:

Blazing Star
Mentzelia laevicaulis

Malvaceae (Mallow Family) Leaves are mostly palmately divided, often bearing hairs branched in star-like pattern (stellate) Flowers have five sepals, five separate petals. Stamens are numerous, fused by filaments into a hollow tube. Ovary is segmented radially like a cheese wheel

If leaves are bluish-green; flowers large, in open racemes, it is
Checkerbloom
Wild Hollyhock
Sidalcea glaucescens

If leaves are green; flowers smaller, in spikes, it is
Checkerbloom
Wild Hollyhock
S. spicata

S. reptans, with creeping stems, also occurs in Sierra.

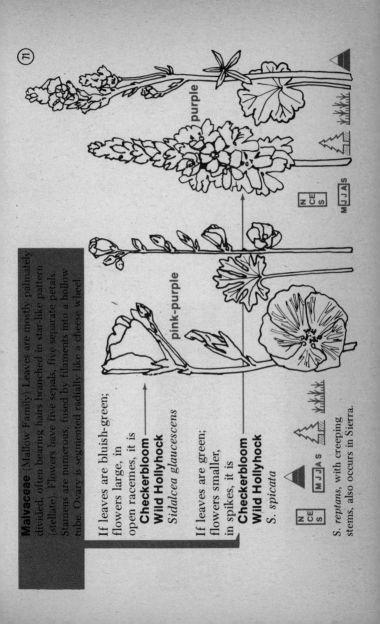

pink-purple

purple

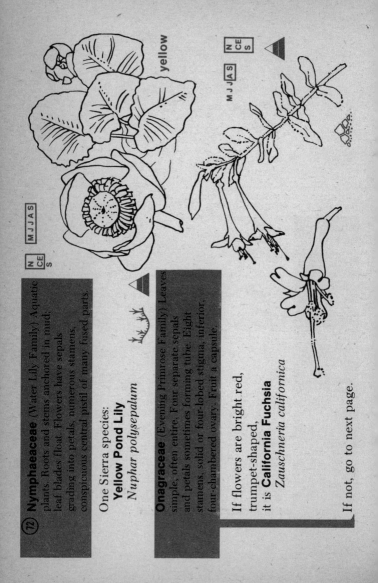

Nymphaeaceae (Water Lily Family) Aquatic plants. Roots and stems anchored in mud; leaf blades float. Flowers have sepals grading into petals, numerous stamens, conspicuous central pistil of many fused parts.

One Sierra species:
Yellow Pond Lily
Nuphar polysepalum

yellow

Onagraceae (Evening Primrose Family) Leaves simple, often entire. Four separate sepals and petals sometimes forming tube. Eight stamens, solid or four-lobed stigma, inferior, four-chambered ovary. Fruit a capsule.

If flowers are bright red, trumpet-shaped, it is **California Fuchsia** *Zauschneria californica*

If not, go to next page.

If flowers are:

● purple to pink,
go to next page.

MJJA s
N
CE
S

● whitish, stems thread-like,
it is **Gayophytum**
Gayophytum nuttallii

A few similar species
also occur in Sierra.

● yellow, with:

  – basal leaves, flowers
  close to ground, it is
  Evening Primrose
  Oenothera heterantha

  – tall, leafy stems, flowers
  above leaves, it is
  Evening Primrose
  O. hookeri

If sepals turn to one side of flower, go to next page.

If sepals are symmetrical, and the plant:

• has tall racemes of flowers, it is **Willow Herb, Fireweed**
  Epilobium angustifolium

Many smaller-flowered, similar-looking willow herbs occur in Sierra: *E. paniculatum, E. glandulosum, E. exaltatum, E. brevistylum, E. pringleanum, E. glaberrimum, E. anagallidifolium, E. hornemannii, E. lactiflorum, E. adenocaulon.*

• forms sprawling mounds, it is **Rockfringe**
  Purple Mats
  E. obcordatum

If flowers are bowl-shaped
with broad petals, it is
Godetia, Farewell-to-spring
Clarkia purpurea

Similar, less common
species occur in Sierra,
especially *C. viminea.*

If flowers have fan-shaped
petals, it is

Purple Fans
C. rhomboidea

Less common species
also occur in Sierra.

N
C ◁ M J J A S
S

N
C ◁ M J J A S
S

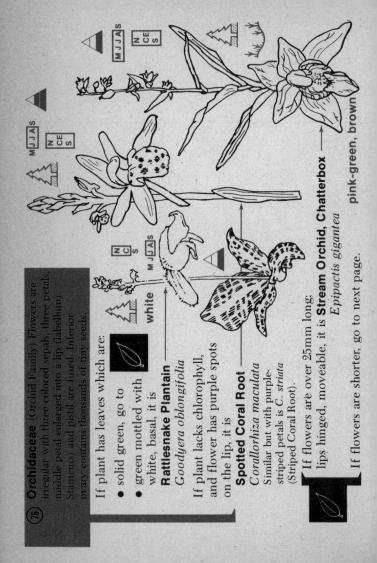

76 **Orchidaceae** (Orchid Family) Flowers are irregular with three colored sepals, three petals, middle petal enlarged into a lip (labellum). Stamen(s) and pistil are fused. Inferior ovary contains thousands of tiny seeds.

If plant has leaves which are:

- solid green, go to
- green mottled with white, basal, it is

Rattlesnake Plantain
Goodyera oblongifolia

If plant lacks chlorophyll, and flower has purple spots on the lip, it is

Spotted Coral Root
Corallorhiza maculata
Similar but with purple-striped petals is *C. striata* (Striped Coral Root).

white

If flowers are over 25mm long; lips hinged, moveable, it is **Stream Orchid, Chatterbox**
Epipactis gigantea → pink-green, brown

If flowers are shorter, go to next page.

If flowers are arranged spirally on a spike, it is

Ladies' Tresses

Spiranthes romanzoffiana

Less common in Sierra is *S. porrifolia*.

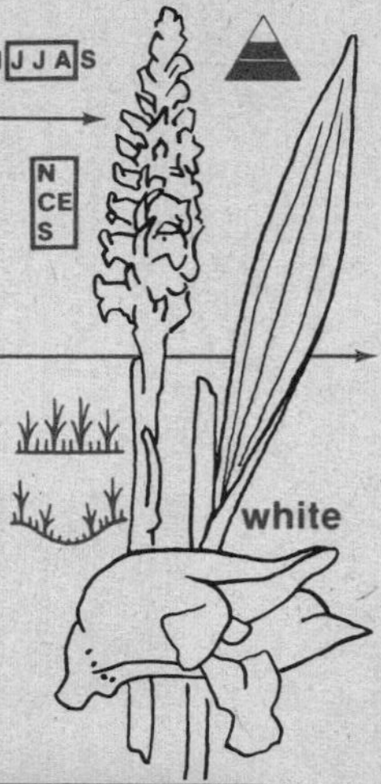

If flowers are spurred, it is

Snowy Rein Orchis

Habenaria dilatata

Also in Sierra: *H. elegans*, small, greenish-white flowers, in dry woods; *H. sparsiflora*, green flowers, in wet spots.

A few very rare orchids are not shown here, including *Cypripedium* (Lady Slipper), and *Listera* (Twayblade).

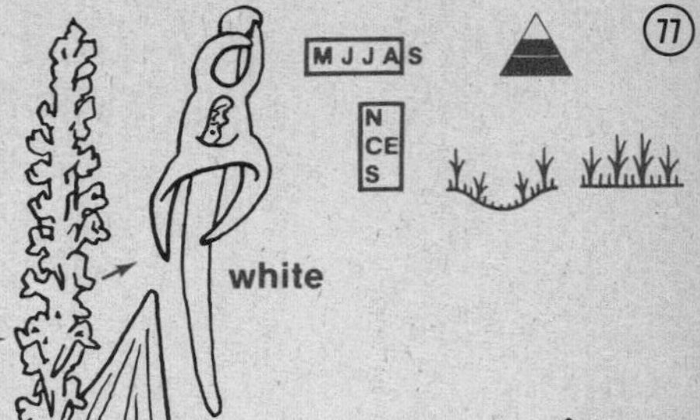

white

white

purple

Orobanchaceae (Broomrape Family) Parasites whose flowers look like figworts. Plants lack chlorophyll, are colored purple, brown or yellowish, have scale-like leaves. Roots parasitize nearby host-plant roots.

Most common Sierra species: **Broomrape**

Orobanche grayana

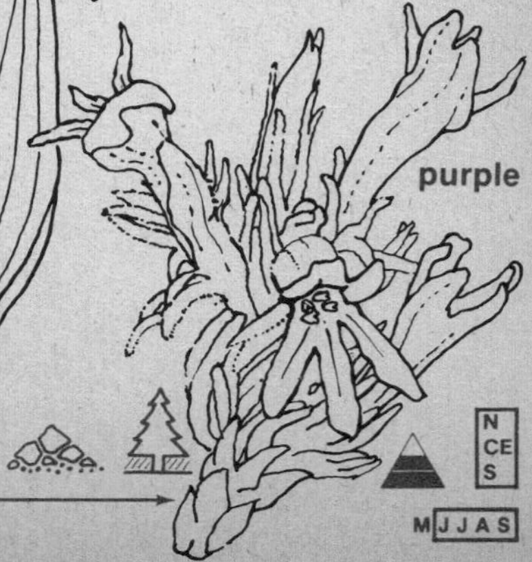

(78) Paeoniaceae (Peony Family)
Closely related to buttercups. Principal difference is direction of development of the numerous stamens, and sepals which remain on flower even in fruit.

One Sierra species: **Wild Peony**
Paeonia brownii
maroon-red

Papaveraceae (Poppy Family) Sepals, which fall as bud opens, are usually half the number of petals. Petals are free, often crinkled, four to six. Stamens are numerous, pistil compound, fruit a capsule.

If leaves are:

● much divided, ferny; flowers orange-yellow, it is
California Poppy
Eschscholzia californica

● very spiny; flowers snowy white, it is
Prickly Poppy
Argemone munita

Polemoniaceae (Phlox Family) Leaves variable. Flower parts are in fives and partly fused, except for three-lobed stigma and three-chambered ovary. Petals are often fused into conspicuous tubes. Fruit a many-seeded capsule.

If leaves are:

- undivided, go to ▢ p. 81

- divided pinnately, go to ▢ →

- divided palmately, go to ▢ p. 81

If leaves smell skunky, or are pinnately compound like pea leaves, go to next page.

If leaves are otherwise; and flowers are:

- red, rose-pink, long, tubular, it is **Sky Rocket, Scarlet Gilia** →
  Ipomopsis aggregata

- whitish, tightly clustered in a head, it is **Wooly Heads**
  I. congesta

• blue, purplish or light pink, go to page 83.

blue-purple   blue-purple   blue-purple

If leaves are
spine-tipped, it is
  Skunkweed
  Navarretia intertexta

Other Sierra species include
N. propinqua and *N. divaricata*.

If leaves lack spines, are
pinnately compound like
pea leaves, and have:

● coarse divisions, it is
  Jacob's Ladder
  Polemonium caeruleum

● fine leaf divisions,
  closely overlapping, it is
  Alpine Jacob's Ladder
  P. pulcherrimum

Others in Sierra: *P. eximium*
(Sky Pilot), leaflets redivided;
and *P. californicum*, three end
leaflets joined at their bases.

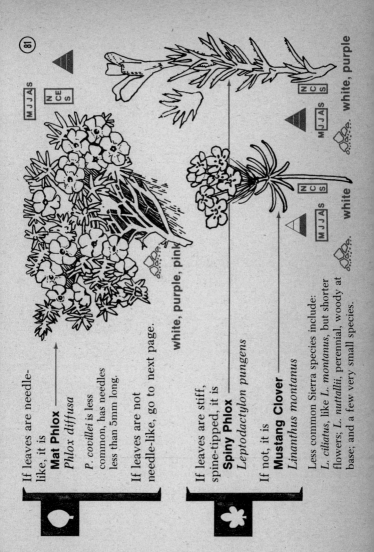

If leaves are needle-like, it is

Mat Phlox
Phlox diffusa

P. covillei is less common, has needles less than 5mm long.

If leaves are not needle-like, go to next page.

white, purple, pink

⎡M J J A⎤s   ⎡N⎤
           ⎢CE⎥
           ⎣S⎦

If leaves are stiff, spine-tipped, it is
Spiny Phlox
Leptodactylon pungens

If not, it is
Mustang Clover
Linanthus montanus

Less common Sierra species include: L. ciliatus, like L. montanus, but shorter flowers; L. nuttallii, perennial, woody at base; and a few very small species.

white, purple

⎡M J J A⎤s   ⎡N⎤
           ⎢C⎥
           ⎣S⎦

white

⎡M J J A⎤s   ⎡N⎤
           ⎢C⎥
           ⎣S⎦

(82)

If plants are woody at base; flowers pinkish, it is

Showy Phlox →
Phlox speciosa

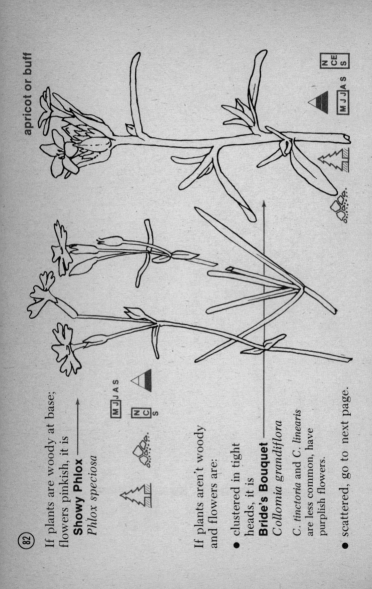

M J A S
N
C
S

If plants aren't woody and flowers are:

• clustered in tight heads, it is
Bride's Bouquet
Collomia grandiflora

C. tinctoria and *C. linearis* are less common, have purplish flowers.

• scattered, go to next page.

N
CE
S
M J J A S

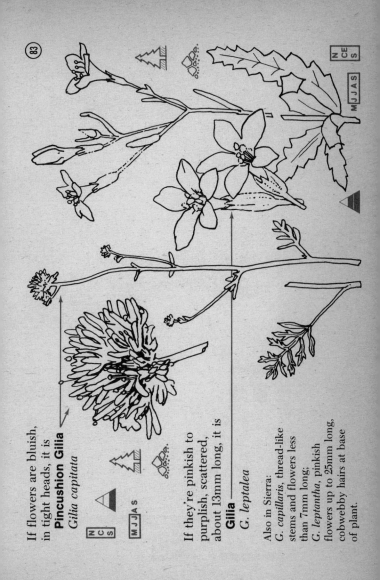

If flowers are bluish,
in tight heads, it is
Pincushion Gilia

Gilia capitata

N
C
S

M J J A S

If they're pinkish to
purplish, scattered,
about 13mm long, it is

Gilia

G. leptalea

Also in Sierra:
G. capillaris, thread-like
stems and flowers less
than 7mm long;
G. leptantha, pinkish
flowers up to 25mm long,
cobwebby hairs at base
of plant.

N
CE
S

M J J A S

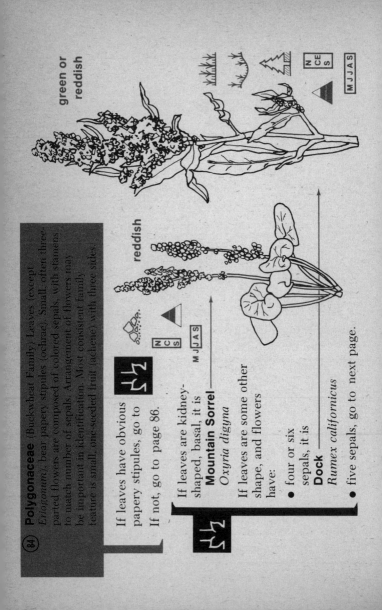

84 **Polygonaceae** (Buckwheat Family) Leaves (except *Eriogonum*), bear papery stipules (ochrea). Small, often three-parted flowers are composed of colored sepals, with stamens to match number of sepals. Arrangement of flowers may be important in identification. Most consistent family feature is small, one-seeded fruit (achene) with three sides.

green or reddish

If leaves have obvious papery stipules, go to

If not, go to page 86.

reddish

If leaves are kidney-shaped, basal, it is
Mountain Sorrel
Oxyria digyna

M J J A S

N
C
S

If leaves are some other shape, and flowers have:

• four or six sepals, it is
Dock
Rumex californicus

• five sepals, go to next page.

If flowers are:

● pink, growing in
  water, it is
  **Water Knotweed
  Smartweed** ———→
  Polygonum coccineum

● white, in dense
  spikes, it is
  Bistort
  P. bistortoides

● greenish, red stems,
  broad leaves, it is
  Green-flowered Knotweed
  P. davisiae

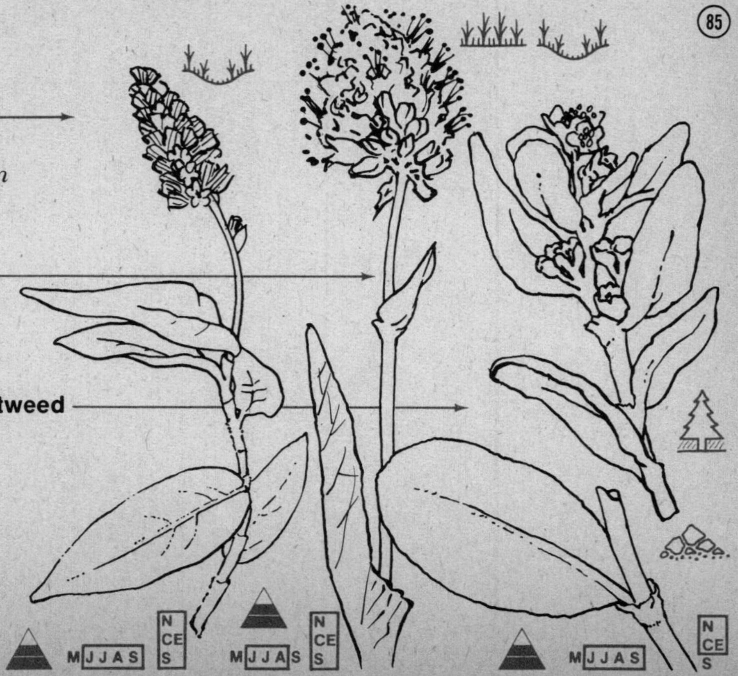

Other Sierra species:
*P. douglasii, P. kelloggii,
P. shastense,
P. phytolaccaefolium.*

If flowers are
yellow, go to next page.

If flowers are
white to pink, and:

● flower clusters are in
ball-like heads with:

– leaves densely matted,
flower stems unbranched,
it is **Alpine Buckwheat**
Eriogonum ovalifolium

– leaves not so tight,
flower stems branched,
it is **Common Buckwheat**
E. nudum

● flower clusters attached singly
on separate small stems, it is
Wright's Buckwheat
E. wrightii

Also in Sierra: *E. spergulinum, E. vimineum.*

If sepals stand up,
it is
Sulfur Flower ⟶
Eriogonum marifolium

If they turn down,
it is
Sulfur Flower
E. umbellatum

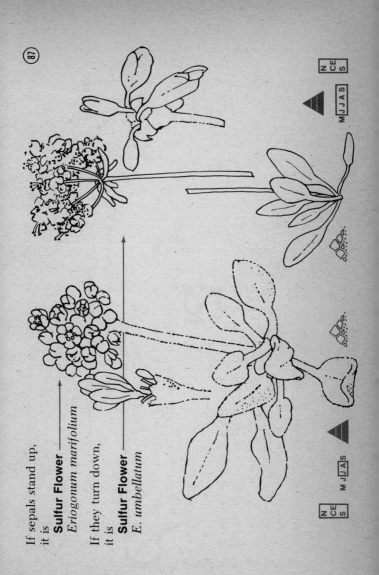

Portulacaceae (Portulaca Family) Leaves are fleshy, often paired. Flowers usually have two sepals, five petals, five stamens. Seeds, produced in capsules, are typically round, shiny, black.

If flowers are striking red-purple, it is **Red Maids** →

Calandrinia ciliata

If they're faded purple, densely massed, it is **Pussy Paws**

Calyptridium umbellatum

If they're not as above, go to →

If there are either more than two sepals and/or more than five petals, and:

● sepals are colored, petal-like, flowers showy, it is **Bitter Root** →

Lewisia rediviva purple, **pink**, white

● sepals are greenish, veined; flowers inconspicuous, it is Pygmy Lewisia (illus. next page).
Others in Sierra: *L. nevadensis,*
L. triphylla, L. sierrae, L. kelloggii.

If there are just two sepals and just five petals, go to next page.

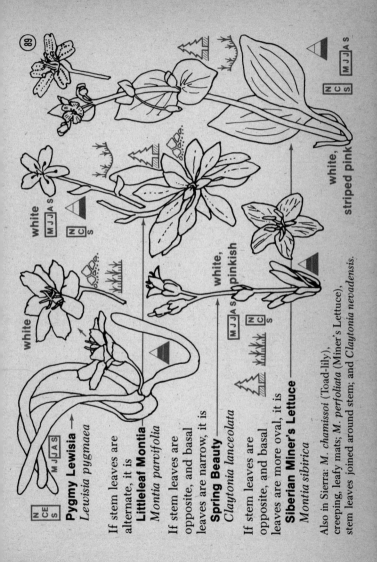

white

M J J A S

Pygmy Lewisia →
Lewisia pygmaea

N
CE
S

M J J A S

If stem leaves are
alternate, it is

Littleleaf Montia
Montia parvifolia

white

M J J A S

N
C
S

If stem leaves are
opposite, and basal
leaves are narrow, it is

Spring Beauty
Claytonia lanceolata

white,
pinkish

M J J A S

N
C
S

If stem leaves are
opposite, and basal
leaves are more oval, it is

Siberian Miner's Lettuce
Montia sibirica

white,
striped pink

N
C
S

M J J A S

Also in Sierra: *M. chamissoi* (Toad-lily),
creeping, leafy mats; *M. perfoliata* (Miner's Lettuce),
stem leaves joined around stem; and *Claytonia nevadensis*.

90) Primulaceae (Primrose Family) Leaves are basal, paired or whorled. Flowers have four to six sepals and petals, fused (sometimes minutely) at bases. Stamens equal petals in number. Fruit a capsule bearing seeds on central column or stalk.

If leaves are: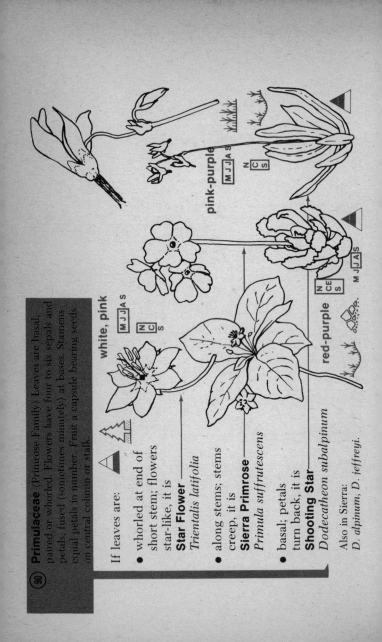

white, pink

● whorled at end of
short stem; flowers
star-like, it is
Star Flower
Trientalis latifolia

● along stems; stems
creep, it is
Sierra Primrose
Primula suffrutescens

pink-purple

● basal; petals
turn back, it is
Shooting Star
Dodecatheon subalpinum

red-purple

Also in Sierra:
D. alpinum, D. jeffreyi.

Pyrolaceae (Wintergreen Family) Herbs adapted to deeply shaded forests with abundant leafmold. Leaves are often variegated with white veins, or are reduced to non-green scales. Roots are coral-like. Plants often sustained by relationship with leafmold fungi. Flowers are often urn-shaped or like inverted bowls. Ovaries form capsules with thousands of dust-like seeds.

If plant has green
leaves, go to next page.

If plant lacks
chlorophyll, go to

If plant is
brownish, it is
Pinedrops
Pterospora andromedea

If it's bright
red, it is
Snowplant
Sarcodes sanguinea

A few rare species of this non-
green group are not included here.

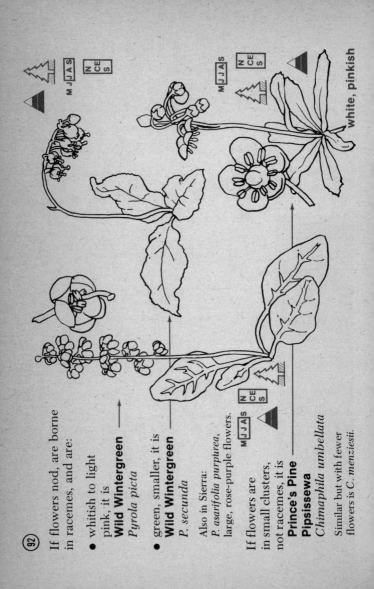

92

If flowers nod, are borne in racemes, and are:

- whitish to light pink, it is
  Wild Wintergreen
  Pyrola picta

- green, smaller, it is
  Wild Wintergreen
  P. secunda

Also in Sierra:
P. asarifolia purpurea, large, rose-purple flowers.

If flowers are in small clusters, not racemes, it is
Prince's Pine
Pipsissewa
Chimaphila umbellata

Similar but with fewer flowers is *C. menziesii.*

white, pinkish

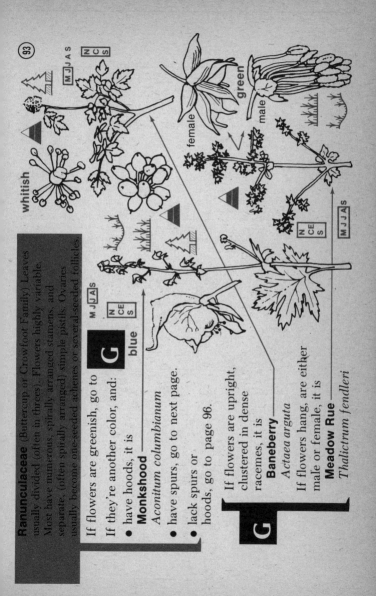

Ranunculaceae (Buttercup or Crowfoot Family) Leaves usually divided (often in threes). Flowers highly variable. Most have numerous, spirally arranged stamens, and separate, (often spirally arranged) simple pistils. Ovaries usually become one-seeded achenes or several-seeded follicles.

If flowers are greenish, go to **G**

If they're another color, and:

- have hoods, it is
  Monkshood blue
  Aconitum columbianum
- have spurs, go to next page.
- lack spurs or
  hoods, go to page 96.

G

If flowers are upright, clustered in dense racemes, it is
  Baneberry
  Actaea arguta

If flowers hang, are either male or female, it is
  Meadow Rue
  Thalictrum fendleri

whitish

green

female

male

93

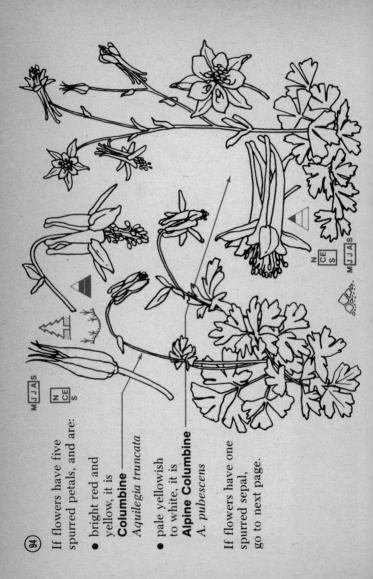

94

If flowers have five
spurred petals, and are:

- bright red and
  yellow, it is
  Columbine
  Aquilegia truncata

- pale yellowish
  to white, it is
  Alpine Columbine
  A. pubescens

If flowers have one
spurred sepal,
go to next page.

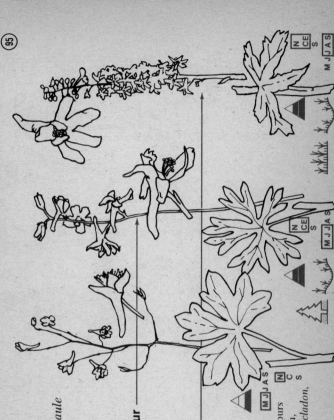

If flowers are:

- red-orange, it is
  Scarlet Larkspur
  Delphinium nudicaule

- pale blue-purple
  with hairy sepals;
  plant less than
  .5m tall, it is
  Mountain Larkspur
  D. depauperatum

- blue; plant over
  .5m tall, it is
  Giant Larkspur
  D. glaucum

Other blue-purple larkspurs
in Sierra: *D. gracilentum,
D. nuttallianum, D. polycladon,
D. pratense, D. sonnei.*

If flowers have non-green sepals, no petals, go to next page.

If there are greenish sepals, brightly colored petals, and plants:

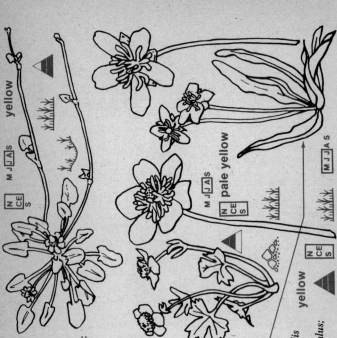

yellow

M J J A S

N CE S

- send out runners to start new plants, it is
Creeping Buttercup
Ramunculus flammula

pale yellow

M J J A S

N CE S

- have toothed, lobed leaves, it is
Alpine Buttercup
R. eschscholtzii

yellow

M J J A S

N CE S

- have untoothed, unlobed leaves, it is
Meadow Buttercup
R. alismaefolius

Also in Sierra: R. aquatilis (Water Buttercup), white flowers; R. occidentalis (Western Buttercup), yellow flowers, deeply divided, hairy leaves; R. hystriculus; R. orthorhynchus; R. cymbalaria.

If flowers are cream-colored (blue in bud); leaves kidney-shaped, it is

Marsh Marigold ⟶
Caltha howellii

If flowers are white, over 5cm across; leaves divided, it is

Western Windflower —
Anemone occidentalis

A. drummondii, smaller flowers, inconspicuous styles in fruit, also occurs in Sierra.

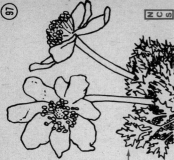

M J J A S

N
C
S

98 **Rosaceae** (Rose Family) A prominent family. Leaves usually compound and bearing stipules. Flowers have five sepals fused at base into cup, five separate petals, usually numerous stamens. Sepals may appear double, due to row of bracts just below which alternate with them. Pistils vary. In herbaceous kinds they're usually several, separate, with superior ovaries.

If leaves are divided into three parts, go to → **3**

If not, go to → **∂**

3

If leaflets have uneven teeth; flowers pale yellow, it is **Sibbaldia**
Sibbaldia procumbens

If teeth are even; flowers white; leaves bluish-green, it is **Mountain Strawberry**
Fragaria platypetala

∂

If plants have woody bases and strong, penetrating odor it is **Mountain Misery** →
Chamaebatia foliolosa

If not, go to next page.

F. californica (Wood Strawberry), green leaves, also occurs in Sierra.

white

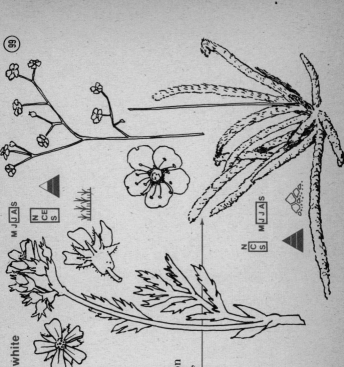

If petals are abruptly
narrowed at their
bases, and leaves are:

- aromatic when crushed,
  it is **Horkelia**
  Horkelia fusca

  H. tridentata is less
  common in Sierra.

- non-aromatic, so finely
  divided they resemble fur on
  a gopher tail; flowers white,
  it is **Rock Potentilla**
  Ivesia santolinoides

Other species in Sierra may
have coarser leaves, and/or
yellow flowers. They include:
*I. pygmaea, I. lycopodioides,
I. gordonii, I. shockleyi,
I. muirii, I. unguiculata.*

If leaves and flowers are
not as above, go to next page.

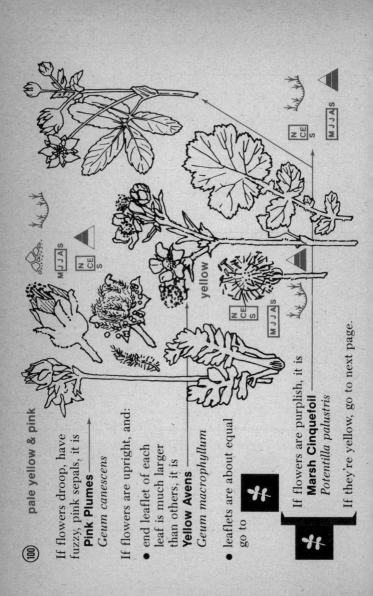

If flowers droop, have
fuzzy, pink sepals, it is
Pink Plumes →
Geum canescens

If flowers are upright, and:

- end leaflet of each
  leaf is much larger
  than others, it is
  Yellow Avens
  Geum macrophyllum

- leaflets are about equal
  go to ✿

If flowers are purplish, it is
Marsh Cinquefoil
Potentilla palustris

If they're yellow, go to next page.

yellow

If flowers are pale yellow or white; leaves with gland-tipped hairs, it is

Sticky Cinquefoil ———→
Potentilla glandulosa

If flowers are bright yellow; and leaves are:

● palmately divided, it is
Meadow Cinquefoil ——
P. gracilis

● pinnately divided, green above, silvery beneath, it is
Silverweed
P. anserina

● pinnately divided with wooly, white hairs, it is
Brewer's Potentilla ———
P. breweri

Also in Sierra: *P. drummondii, P. flabellifolia, P. diversifolia, P. pseudosericea.*

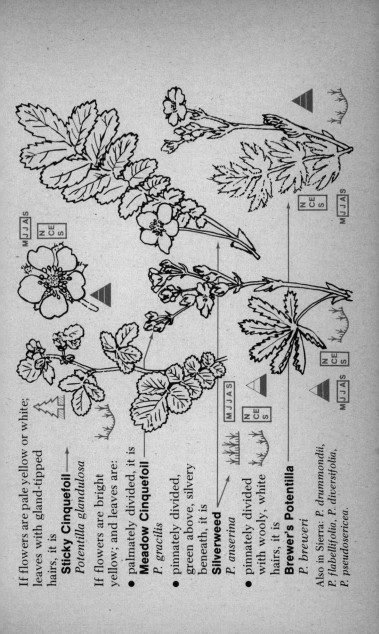

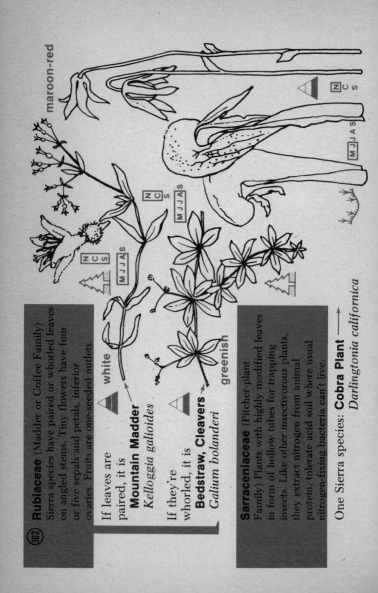

maroon-red

102 **Rubiaceae** (Madder or Coffee Family) Sierra species have paired or whorled leaves on angled stems. Tiny flowers have four or five sepals and petals, inferior ovaries. Fruits are one-seeded nutlets.

If leaves are paired, it is **Mountain Madder** ◢ white *Kelloggia galioides*

If they're whorled, it is **Bedstraw, Cleavers** ◢ greenish *Galium bolanderi*

Sarraceniaceae (Pitcher-plant Family) Plants with highly modified leaves in form of hollow tubes for trapping insects. Like other insectivorous plants, they extract nitrogen from animal protein, tolerate acid soil where usual nitrogen-fixing bacteria can't live.

One Sierra species: **Cobra Plant** ⟶ *Darlingtonia californica*

Saxifragaceae (Saxifrage Family) Flowers have four to five sepals fused at bases into a cup, four to five free petals, five or ten stamens. Ovaries are partly to fully fused, superior to half-inferior. Saxifrages are hard to distinguish from roses except for leaves which are simple, lack stipules and often grow clumped in basal rosettes. Fruit is several-seeded capsule.

If leaves are large, umbrella-like, it is **Indian Rhubarb**
Peltiphyllum peltatum

If not, and petals are:
- slashed or fringed, go to
- undivided, go to next page.

If flowers are white to pink, it is **Woodland Star**
Lithophragma bulbifera

L. heterophylla and *L. breviloba* may occur at lower elevations.

If they're small, green, it is **Mitrewort, Bishop's Cap**
Mitella pentandra

white to pink

(103)

If leaves are coarsely
scalloped or lobed,
go to

If not (although they
may be toothed), go to next page.

If flowers hang, and are:

- green and dull
  purple, it is
  Bolander
  Bolandra californica

- white to pink, it is
  Alumroot
  Heuchera rubescens

If flowers are face up,
star-like, it is
Brook Saxifrage
Boykinia elata

B. major, larger flowers and
leaves, petals 5 to 7mm long,
also occurs in Sierra.

MJJAS

N
CE
S

MJJAS

N
CE
S

MJJAS

N
C
S

white

(105)

If flowers have five pollen-bearing stamens and several gland-tipped, sterile stamens, it is **Grass of Parnassus** → *Parnassia palustris*

P. fimbriata, fringed petals, also occurs.

If flowers have ten pollen-bearing stamens (no sterile ones), and:

- leaves are rounded, with coarse teeth, it is
  Spotted Saxifrage
  Saxifraga punctata

- leaves are elliptical, without teeth, it is
  Meadow Saxifrage
  S. oregana

- bulblets replace some flowers; parts tiny, it is
  Moss Saxifrage →
  S. bryophora

Also in Sierra: *S. tolmiei*, *S. fallax*, *S. mertensiana*.

white

M J [J] A s

N
C
S

white

M J J A s

N
CE
S

white

N
CE
S

white

M J [A] s

N
CE
S

106 **Scrophulariaceae** (Figwort or Snapdragon Family) A large, important family. Flowers mostly irregular with upper lip of two petals, lower lip of three. All petals fused into tube below. Stamens usually two to five. Stigma often two-lobed, ovary two-chambered, fruit a many-seeded capsule. Some scrophs with square stems and opposite leaves resemble mints, but lack mint aroma.

If there are bracts as long as or longer than flowers, sometimes brightly colored, go to

If bracts are shorter, or are missing, and flowers are:

• irregular, obviously two-lipped, go to next page.

• nearly regular, not two-lipped, go to page 114.

If petals are easy to find, brightly colored, not green, go to page 108.

If petals are green, partly hidden by sepals and bracts, and bracts are:

• pinkish to purplish, it is **Meadow Paintbrush** ———→
  Castilleia lemmonii

• greenish; flowers whitish, it is **Alpine Paintbrush** ——→
  C. nana

Other Sierra species with yellow, orange or red bracts include:
  C. culbertsonii, C. breweri, C. applegatei, C. miniata.

If maroon-brown upper lip
arches like a hood beyond
lower lip, it is;
Figwort
Scrophularia californica

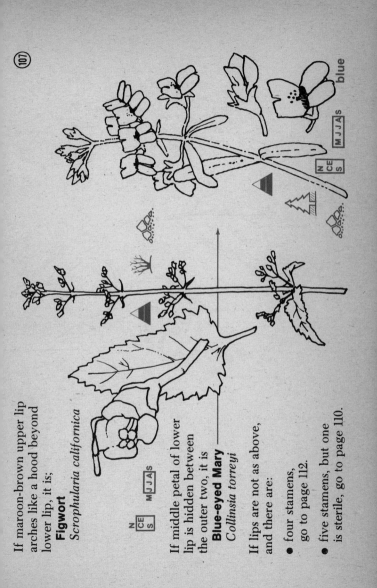

If middle petal of lower
lip is hidden between
the outer two, it is
Blue-eyed Mary
Collinsia torreyi

If lips are not as above,
and there are:

● four stamens,
go to page 112.

● five stamens, but one
is sterile, go to page 110.

blue

If flowers are scattered; petals with lower lip white, it is

Pelican Flower →
Cordylanthus tenuis

Other hard to tell apart species occur.

If flowers are in dense racemes or spikes, and have:

- sac-like (inflated) lower lips, hooked upper lips, and are:

  – white and purple, it is
  Owl's Clover
  Orthocarpus copelandii

  – bright yellow, it is
  Mountain Cream Sacs
  O. lacerus

- hatchet-shaped or snout-like upper lips,
  go to next page.

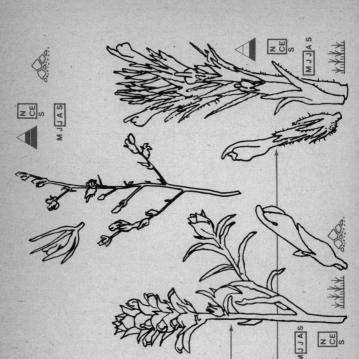

If flowers are:

- dull yellow, it is
  Indian Warrior
  Pedicularis semibarbata

- purple, with long,
  snout-like upper
  lip, it is
  Elephant Snouts
  P. groenlandica

P. attolens, shorter
with uncurled "snout"
also occurs in Sierra.

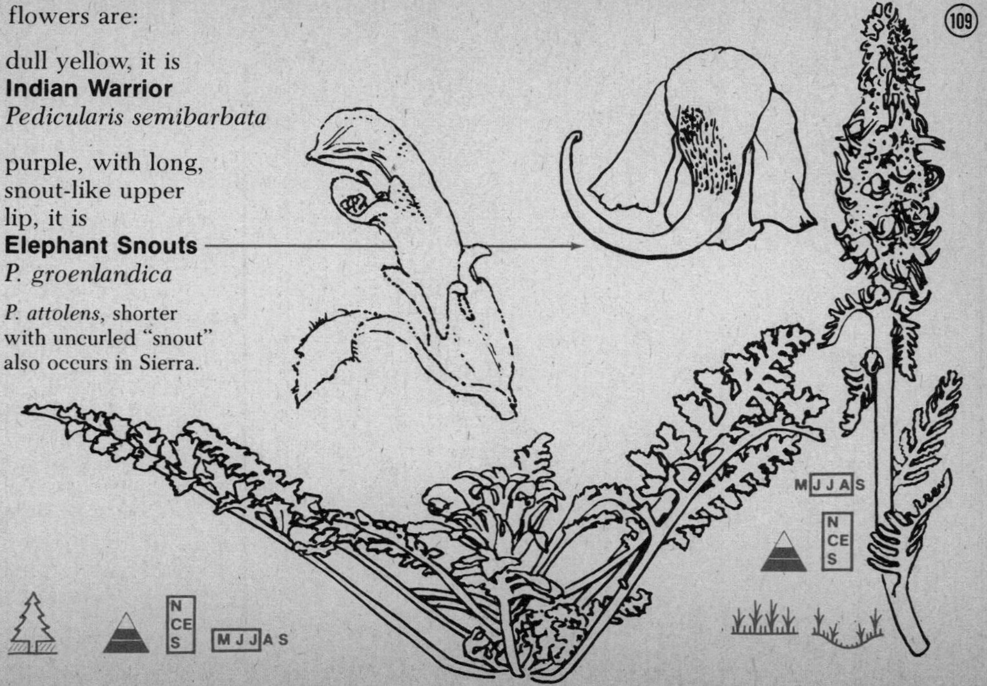

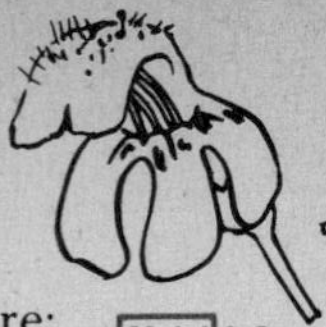

110

▲ N CE S   M J J A s

If flowers are:

- white, with gaping petals, it is
  Gaping Beard-tongue
  Penstemon breviflorus

  P. deustus, white flowers, clustered; petals not gaping, also occurs in Sierra

- bright red, it is
  Red Penstemon
  P. bridgesii

- rose-purple, it is
  Mountain Pride
  P. newberryi

▲ N C S   M J J A s

- blue-purple, go to next page.

(111)

If plants are in low
mats, it is
Mat Penstemon
Penstemon davidsonii

If plants are upright, and:

- flowers are whorled, it is
  Meadow Beard-tongue
  P. procerus

- flowers are in small clusters,
  large, it is
  Showy Blue Penstemon
  P. speciosus

Other Sierra species, most with blue-purple
flowers: *P. azureus, P. heterodoxus, P. laetus
P. gracilentus, P. heterophyllus.*

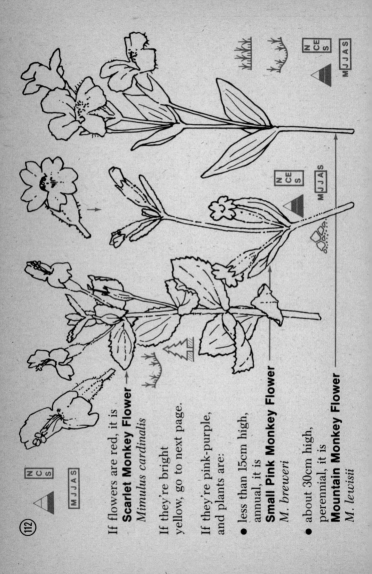

112

If flowers are red, it is
Scarlet Monkey Flower
Mimulus cardinalis

If they're bright
yellow, go to next page.

If they're pink-purple,
and plants are:

● less than 15cm high,
annual, it is
Small Pink Monkey Flower
M. breweri

● about 30cm high,
perennial, it is
Mountain Monkey Flower
M. lewisii

If leaves are slimy, it is
Musk Monkey Flower
Mimulus moschatus

If not, and flowers are:

- large, brown-spotted, in racemes, it is
Golden Monkey Flower
M. guttatus

- small, borne singly on stems; leaves edged with white hairs, it is
Primrose-flowered Monkey Flower
M. primuloides

Like *M. primuloides*, but with skunky odor is *M. mephiticus.*

Other *Mimulus* species in Sierra: *M. suksdorfii; M. grayi, M. bicolor, M. discolor, M. floribundus, M. arenarius, M. laciniatus, M. leptaleus, M. nasutus, M. tilingii.*

If flowers are blue-purple; stamens two; stems creeping, it is

Speedwell
American Brooklime
Veronica americana

Other Sierra species, most with upright stems, include: *V. alpina, V. serpyllifolia, V. peregrina, V. scutellata.*

If flowers are yellow; stamens five, it is

Common Mullein
Verbascum thapsus

| M J J A S |
| N |
| CE |
| S |

Solanaceae (Tomato, Potato or Nightshade Family) Flowers have five partly fused sepals, five mostly fused petals, sometimes pleated in bud; also five stamens which sometimes stick together. Fruit a capsule or many-seeded berry.

One Sierra species: **Blue Witch**
Blue Nightshade
Solanum xantii

| M J J A S |
| N |
| CE |
| S |

blue-purple

Umbelliferae (Carrot, Parsley or Umbel Family) Leaves are usually compound or divided, form sheaths around stem at bases, have characteristic odors when crushed. Flowers are in compound umbels, mostly small greenish, yellow or white. Inferior ovary splits into two one-seeded segments in fruit. Some species are deadly poisonous, others edible.

If umbels have tight, head-like clusters, go to

If not, and flowers are:

● greenish or yellow, go to **GY** next page

● white, go to **W** next page

If flowers are yellow, it is
Sanicle
Sanicula tuberosa
S. *graveolens* also occurs in Sierra.

If they're white, it is
White Heads, Ranger's Buttons
Sphenosciadium capitellatum

116

Gy

If flowers are greenish, foliage licorice-scented, it is

Sweet Cicely
Osmorhiza occidentalis
Also in Sierra: *O. chilensis*, *O. brachypoda*.

If flowers are yellow, go to **Y**

Y

If leaves are green, it is

Biscuit Root
Lomatium torreyi
Less common in Sierra: *L. nudicaule*, *L. nevadense* (white flowers).

If they're grey-green, it is *Pteryxia terebinthina*, not illustrated.

W

If plants are in or next to water, go to next page.

If not, and:

- leaves have few, coarse divisions, go to → p. 118
- leaves have several fine, often narrow divisions, go to → p. 118

If leaves are divided several
times, so that divisions have
divisions, at least at their
lower parts, it is
Water Hemlock
Cicuta douglasii

Water Hemlock is deadly poisonous.
Upper roots are chambered inside.

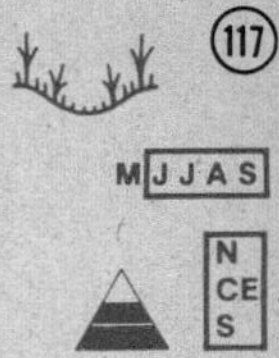

If leaves are only once
divided, and leaflets are:

- paired, 10 to 18, it is
  ### Oxypolis
  Oxypolis occidentalis

- not paired, of an odd
  number, 5 to 13, it is
  ### Water Parsnip
  Berula erecta

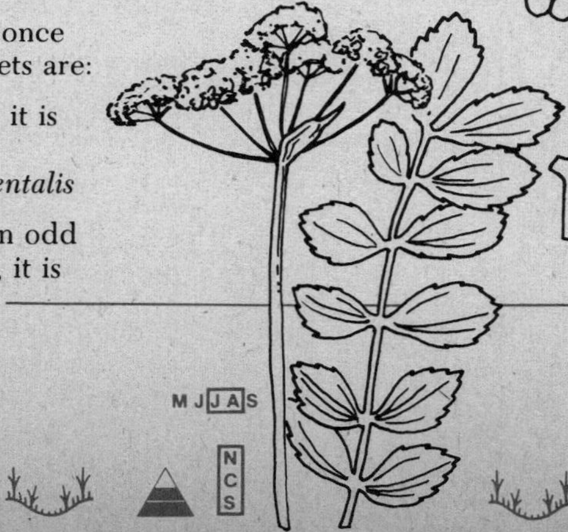

(118)

If leaves are divided into
a few uneven, ragged segments;
flowering stalks often
over 1.3m tall, it is
Cow Parsnip
Heracleum lanatum

If leaves are divided into
more than six symmetrical
segments, it is
Angelica
Angelica breweri

A. *lineariloba*, very narrow, long
leaflets, also occurs in Sierra.

If leaf divisions are widely
separated; plants growing from
tubers, it is Yampah. See next page.

If leaf divisions are broad,
often in threes, it is
Mountain Lovage
Ligusticum grayi

(*Also check Lomatium*, p. 116.)

Yampah
Perideridia gairdneri

Less common in Sierra: *P. bolanderi*,
P. parishii. If your specimen is over
1m tall, it may be *Angelica*. See above.

Valerianaceae (Valerian Family) Opposite,
leaves. Five sepals, often fringed, five
partly-fused petals with a small sac or spur to one
side. Flowers are slightly to definitely irregular.
Ovary inferior, fruit a one-seeded achene.

One Sierra species: **Mountain Valerian**
Valeriana capitata

white

(120) Violaceae (Violet Family) Five petals, five sepals. Lower middle petal has nectar-bearing spur. Five stamens are at entrance to throat. Ovary forms three-sided capsule which explodes to discharge seeds.

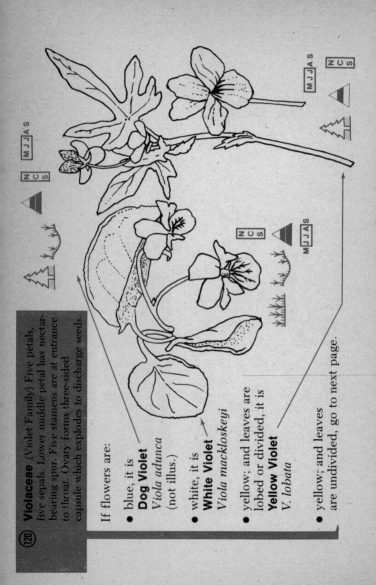

If flowers are:

- blue, it is
  Dog Violet
  Viola adunca
  (not illus.)

- white, it is
  White Violet
  Viola mackloskeyi

- yellow; and leaves are
  lobed or divided, it is
  Yellow Violet
  V. lobata

- yellow; and leaves
  are undivided, go to next page.

If leaves are:

● heart-shaped, green, it is
  Pine Violet
  Viola purpurea

● narrower, white-haired, it is
  Fuzzy Violet →
  V. tomentosa

Other yellow violets in Sierra: *V. glabella*, *V. sheltonii*.

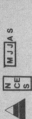

N C E S

M J J A S

N C S

M J J A S

Redwood Region Flower Finder

by Phoebe Watts

illustrated by Sarah Ellen Watts

This book is for identifying wildflowers growing in the range of the Redwood tree (*Sequoia sempervirens*). Flowering trees and shrubs, and plants growing on sea bluffs and beaches, are not included.

M.T.W.

terms that describe flowers

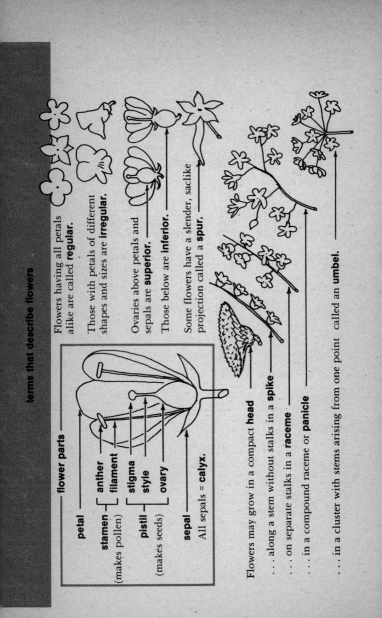

flower parts

petal

stamen { **anther** — **filament** }
(makes pollen)

pistil { **stigma** — **style** — **ovary** }
(makes seeds)

sepal

All sepals = **calyx.**

Flowers having all petals alike are called **regular.**

Those with petals of different shapes and sizes are **irregular.**

Ovaries above petals and sepals are **superior.**

Those below are **inferior.**

Some flowers have a slender, saclike projection called a **spur.**

Flowers may grow in a compact **head**

. . . along a stem without stalks in a **spike**

. . . on separate stalks in a **raceme**

. . . in a compound raceme or **panicle**

. . . in a cluster with stems arising from one point called an **umbel.**

terms that describe plants

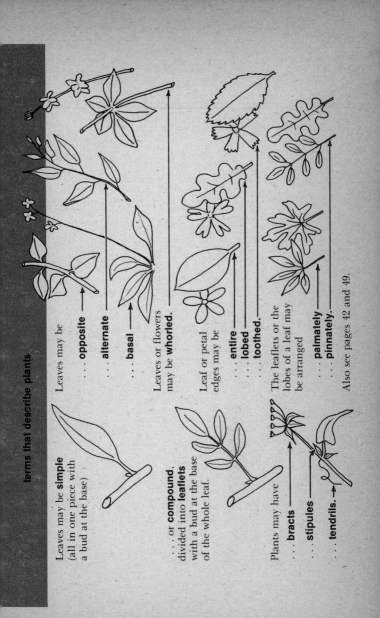

Leaves may be **simple** (all in one piece with a bud at the base)

. . . or **compound**, divided into **leaflets** with a bud at the base of the whole leaf.

Leaves may be

. . . **opposite**

. . . **alternate**

. . . **basal**

Leaves or flowers may be **whorled**.

Leaf or petal edges may be

. . . **entire**

. . . **lobed**

. . . **toothed**.

The leaflets or the lobes of a leaf may be arranged

. . . **palmately**

. . . **pinnately**.

Plants may have

. . . **bracts**

. . . **stipules**

. . . **tendrils**.

Also see pages 42 and 49.

to use this book

Begin on the next page with the first choice: either █ or ☐ and follow directions.

about this book

Habitat symbols show the kinds of places within the redwood region where you're most likely to find each flower.

shady forest

edge of forest

open places

wet places

The months when each plant will probably bloom are printed next to each picture.

jun-aug

You may want a hand lens to see some features used for identification in this key. Wilderness-supply or stamp collectors' stores sell them.

plant names

Common names are printed like this:

Fireweed

The Latin name is printed like this:

Epilobium angustifolium.

The first part of the Latin name is the genus (plural: genera). The second part is the species — the kind of plant within the genus. Related genera are grouped in families. Some common characteristics, and the Latin family name, are given for the plant families with more than one species in this book. Families with only one species in this book are named underneath the Latin name for that plant.

Illustrations are based in part on photographs by Dick Anderson and Glenn Keator.

Begin here.

If the plant has green parts, go to ⟶ ▇ below

If the plant has no green parts, go to ⟶ ☐ below

If the main veins of the leaves are parallel to each other, go to ⟶ page 3

If the main veins form a net-like pattern, go to ⟶

If there is a mass of tightly packed, stemless, small flowers, which altogether look like one flower, go to SUNFLOWER FAMILY, page 42.

If the flowers are not as above, go to ⟶ page 15

If flowers are irregular, go to ⟶ next page

If flowers are regular, go to INDIAN PIPE FAMILY, next page.

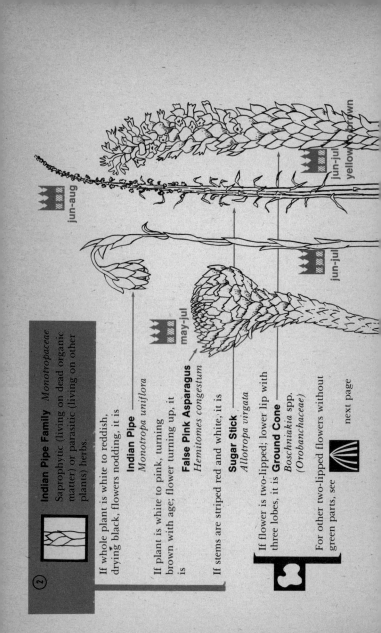

② **Indian Pipe Family** *Monotropaceae*
Saprophytic (living on dead organic matter) or parasitic (living on other plants) herbs.

If whole plant is white to reddish, drying black, flowers nodding, it is
Indian Pipe
Monotropa uniflora

If plant is white to pink, turning brown with age; flower turning up, it is
False Pink Asparagus
Hemitomes congestum

If stems are striped red and white, it is
Sugar Stick
Allotropa virgata

If flower is two-lipped; lower lip with three lobes, it is **Ground Cone**
Boschniakia spp.
(*Orobanchaceae*)

For other two-lipped flowers without green parts, see

next page

jun-aug

jun-jul
yellow to brown

jun-jul

may-jul

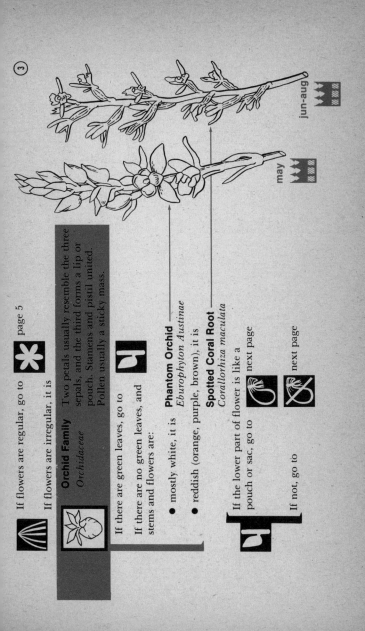

If flowers are regular, go to ✱ page 5

If flowers are irregular, it is

Orchid Family
Orchidaceae

Two petals usually resemble the three sepals, and the third forms a lip or pouch. Stamens and pistil united. Pollen usually a sticky mass.

If there are green leaves, go to

If there are no green leaves, and stems and flowers are:

• mostly white, it is

Phantom Orchid
Eburophyton Austinae

• reddish (orange, purple, brown), it is

Spotted Coral Root
Corallorhiza maculata

If the lower part of flower is like a pouch or sac, go to next page

If not, go to next page

may

jun-aug

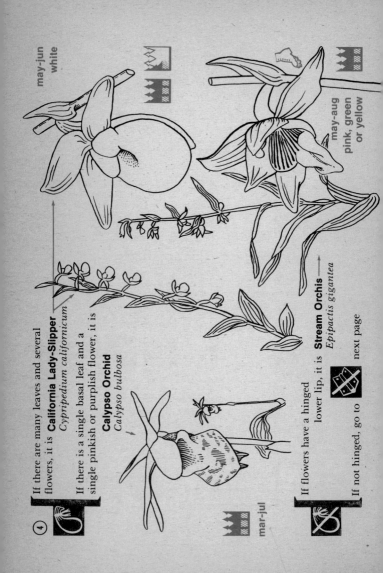

④

If there are many leaves and several flowers, it is **California Lady-Slipper**
Cypripedium californicum

If there is a single basal leaf and a single pinkish or purplish flower, it is
Calypso Orchid
Calypso bulbosa

mar-jul

If flowers have a hinged lower lip, it is **Stream Orchis** →
Epipactis gigantea

If not hinged, go to   next page

may-jun
white

may-aug
pink, green
or yellow

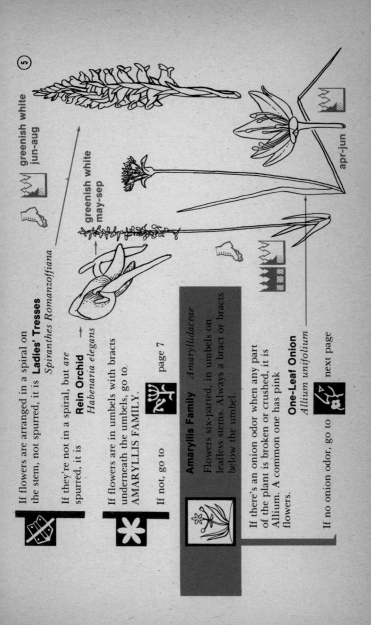

If flowers are arranged in a spiral on the stem, not spurred, it is **Ladies' Tresses**
Spiranthes Romanzoffiana

greenish white
jun-aug

If they're not in a spiral, but *are* spurred, it is
Rein Orchid
Habenaria elegans

greenish white
may-sep

If flowers are in umbels with bracts underneath the umbels, go to AMARYLLIS FAMILY.

If not, go to page 7

Amaryllis Family *Amaryllidaceae*

Flowers six-parted, in umbels on leafless stems. Always a bract or bracts below the umbel.

One-Leaf Onion
Allium unifolium

If there's an onion odor when any part of the plant is broken or crushed, it is Allium. A common one has pink flowers.

If no onion odor, go to next page

apr-jun

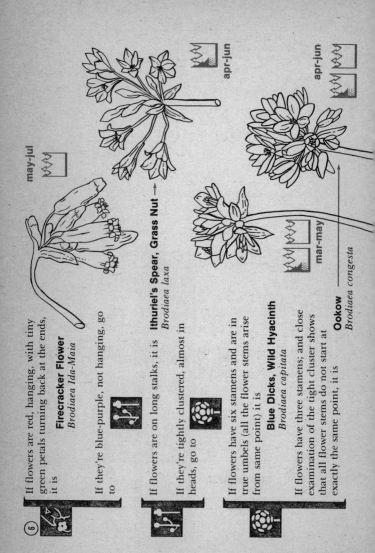

⑥

If flowers are red, hanging, with tiny green petals turning back at the ends, it is

Firecracker Flower
Brodiaea Ida-Maia

may-jul

If they're blue-purple, not hanging, go to

If flowers are on long stalks, it is

Ithuriel's Spear, Grass Nut
Brodiaea laxa

apr-jun

If they're tightly clustered, almost in heads, go to

If flowers have six stamens and are in true umbels (all the flower stems arise from same point) it is

Blue Dicks, Wild Hyacinth
Brodiaea capitata

mar-may

If flowers have three stamens; and close examination of the tight cluster shows that all flower stems do not start at exactly the same point, it is

Ookow
Brodiaea congesta

apr-jun

If leaves overlap on one plane (run your fingers to the base of leaves to feel this) go to IRIS FAMILY.

If not, go to LILY FAMILY, next page.

Iris Family *Iridaceae*

Leaves mostly basal, flowers at ends of stems, above a spathe of bracts which conceal inferior ovary. Stamens three, wide and flat; three-parted stigma.

If petals and sepals are shaped alike, it is

Blue-Eyed Grass
Sisyrinchium bellum

If they're shaped differently, it is Iris. One commonly found in this area is

Wild Iris
Iris Douglasiana

mar-may
blue, purple, yellow or white

Lily Family *Liliaceae*
Leaves usually have main veins parallel. Flower parts in threes or sixes, rarely fours. Petals and sepals often alike. Superior ovary.

If petals and sepals are alike, go to ✳ page 10

If petals differ from sepals, go to ✴

If there is a whorl of three stem leaves, and the flower is:

- on a stalk; it is
  Wake Robin
  Trillium ovatum

- unstalked; it is
  Giant Trillium
  Trillium chloropetalum

If leaves are all or mostly basal, and:
- they're mottled, it is
  Foetid Adder's Tongue, Slinkpod
  Scoliopus Bigelovii

- they're unmottled, go to ▤ next page

feb-apr
white, red

feb-may
white, red, green

feb-mar
dark red

apr-jun
yellow

If flowers are hanging, it is **Fairy Lanterns, Golden Globe Tulip**
Calochortus amabilis

If they face up, go to

If petals are covered with hairs, blue-
purple, it is **Pussy Ears**
Calochortus Tolmiei

If petals are mostly smooth and are
yellow, it is **Mariposa Tulip**
Calochortus luteus

apr-jul

apr-jun

(10)

If leaves grow on stems, go to  page 12

If leaves are basal, or attached very near the ground, go to

If flowers are dark: red, blue or purple, go to ■ next page

If they're pale: white, cream, pale pink, and:

- leaves are light-mottled; flower white to cream with a yellow stripe, it is **Fawn Lily** apr-may
  Erythronium californicum
  (Flower pink, it's *E. revolutum* or *E. oregonum*)

- leaves have wavy margins; flower open only early morning and late day, it is **Soap Plant**
  Chlorogalum pomeridianum

- leaves are narrow, grasslike, with dry, splitting edges, it is
  Bear Grass
  Xerophyllum tenax

- leaves have smooth edges, it is **Star Lily**
  Zigadenus Fremontii

white
may-aug

may-jul
white

next page

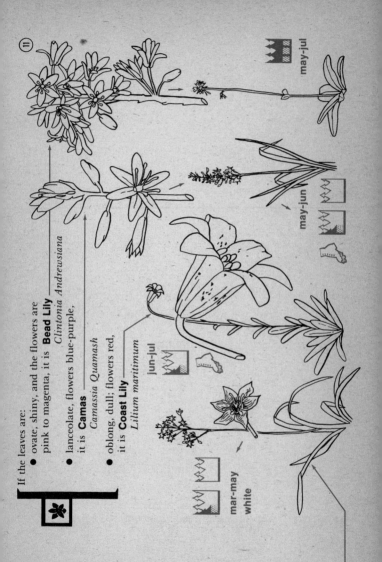

⑪

If the leaves are:

- ovate, shiny, and the flowers are
  pink to magenta, it is **Bead Lily**
  Clintonia Andrewsiana

- lanceolate, flowers blue-purple,
  it is **Camas**
  Camassia Quamash

- oblong, dull; flowers red,
  it is **Coast Lily**
  Lilium maritimum

may-jul

may-jun

jun-jul

mar-may
white

⑫ If some or all of the leaves grow in whorls, go to ⟶ page 14

If not, go to

If petals and sepals turn outward or curl back, go to

If not, it is **Checker Lily, Mission Bells**
Fritillaria lanceolata

If flowers are white to pink, go to

If they're yellow to orange to red, go to next page

If flowers hang, it is
Kellogg's Lily
Lilium Kelloggii

If they're upright, it is
Redwood Lily
Lilium rubescens

jun-jul
pink

feb-may
dark red
with yellow

jun-jul
white aging to purple

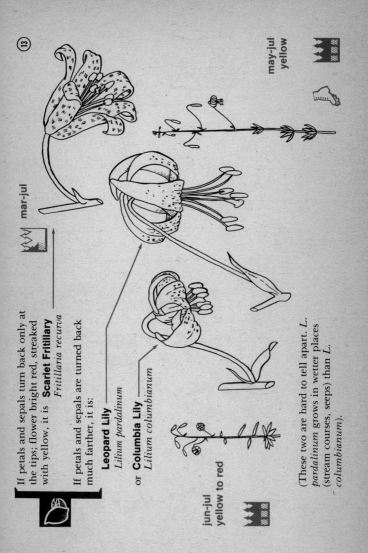

mar-jul

If petals and sepals turn back only at the tips; flower bright red, streaked with yellow, it is **Scarlet Fritillary**
Fritillaria recurva

If petals and sepals are turned back much farther, it is:

Leopard Lily
Lilium pardalinum

or **Columbia Lily**
Lilium columbianum

may-jul yellow

jun-jul yellow to red

(These two are hard to tell apart. *L. pardalinum* grows in wetter places (stream courses, seeps) than *L. columbianum*).

⑭

If flowers are four-parted, it is **False Lily-of-the-Valley** →
Maianthemum dilatatum

may-jun
white

If they're six-parted, go to

If flowers hang, it is
Fairy Bells
Disporum Hookeri

mar-may
white

If they're upright, go to

If flowers are fringed, it is
Fringed Corn Lily →
Veratrum fimbriatrum

If not, go to

next page

white
jul-sep

If flowers are in small racemes, it is
Slim False Solomon's Seal →
Smilacina stellata

If they're in large panicles, it is
Fat False Solomon's Seal
Smilacina racemosa

mar-may
white

mar-may
white

If flowers have numerous stamens
go to

If there are fewer stamens (rarely more
than twice the total of petals and
sepals) go to page 19

apr-sep

If plant grows in water, with large,
bright-yellow flowers, floating leaves, it
is **Yellow Pond Lily**
Nuphar polysepalum
(Nymphaeaceae)

If not, go to next page

⑮

16

If stamens are united by their filaments into a sheath around the pistil, the whole forming a club-like center, it is **Mallow, Cheeses** — *Malva neglecta* (Malvaceae)

(Fruit is like little wheel)

may-oct
lilac, white

If stamens are separate, go to

If sepals are united at their bases to form a calyx tube to which petals and stamens are attached, go to ROSE FAMILY.

If sepals, petals and stamens are all separate, go to next page

Rose Family *Rosaceae*
Leaves usually alternate, with stipules. Flowers regular. Sepals and petals at edge of a flower tube which is lined with a glandular disc.

If leaves are three-parted; flowers white, it is **Woodland Strawberry** — *Fragaria californica*

mar-jun

If leaves are five- to nine-parted; flowers creamy to white-yellow, it is **Sticky Potentilla** — *Potentilla glandulosa*

may-jul

If there is one pistil, go to  page 19

If there are several distinct pistils, it is

Buttercup or Crowfoot Family
Ranunculaceae
Leaves vary greatly. Petals may be lacking, and sepals petaloid; petals or sepals may be spurred. Stamens many. Pistils usually many; ovaries superior.

If flowers have spurs, go to

If not, go to

If flower is horizontal, with one spur, it is **Larkspur**
Delphinium nudicaule

If flower hangs, with five spurs, it is **Columbine**
Aquilegia formosa

jun-aug
red and yellow

If plant is a climbing vine, it is **Clematis**
Clematis ligusticifolia

white
mar-aug

If not a vine, go to next page

mar-jun
red

If flowers are white, go to ❄

If they're shiny yellow, it's a buttercup.
Many kinds grow in the area; the one
pictured is **Buttercup** ⟶
Ranunculus californicus

feb-may

apr-may

If flowers are tiny (4-6 mm), in
racemes, it is **Baneberry**
Actaea rubra, spp. arguta
(Many pistils are joined into one
compound pistil.)

If they're larger (15-30 mm), grow
singly, it is **Windflower** ⟶
Anemone quinquefolia

may-jun

18

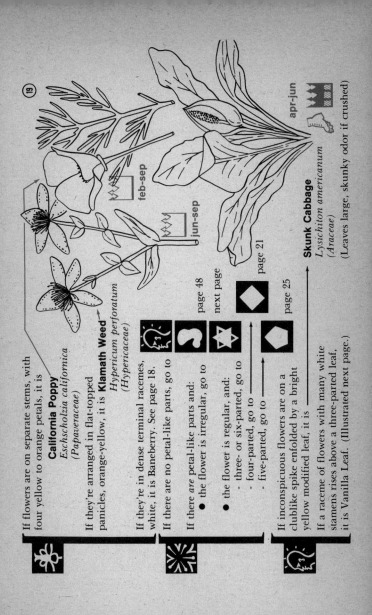

If flowers are on separate stems, with four yellow to orange petals, it is
California Poppy
Eschscholzia californica
(*Papaveraceae*)

If they're arranged in flat-topped panicles, orange-yellow, it is **Klamath Weed**
Hypericum perforatum
(*Hypericaceae*)

If they're in dense terminal racemes, white, it is Baneberry. See page 18.

If there are no petal-like parts, go to page 48

If there *are* petal-like parts and:

• the flower is irregular, go to next page

• the flower is regular, and:
  - three- or six-parted, go to page 21
  - four-parted, go to
  - five-parted, go to page 25

If inconspicuous flowers are on a clublike spike enfolded by a bright yellow modified leaf, it is
Skunk Cabbage
Lysichiton americanum
(*Araceae*)
(Leaves large, skunky odor if crushed)

If a raceme of flowers with many white stamens rises above a three-parted leaf, it is Vanilla Leaf. (Illustrated next page.)

feb-sep

jun-sep

apr-jun

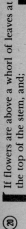

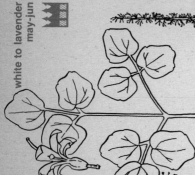

white to lavender
may-jun

white
apr-jun

If flowers are above a whorl of leaves at the top of the stem, and;

- flowers have three petals, go to page 8
- flowers have six petals, go to PRIMROSE FAMILY, page 41.

If six petals sweep strongly backward, go to BARBERRY FAMILY.

If there are three petal-like maroon-colored sepals, go to BIRTHWORT FAMILY, next page.

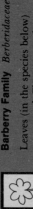

Barberry Family *Berberidaceae*

Leaves (in the species below) compound. Flowers regular.

If leaves are basal; leaflets barely three-lobed, glossy; flowers 6-8 mm long; it is
Redwood Ivy, Inside-Out Flower ⇗
Vancouveria planipetala

(Leaves not glossy, flowers 10-14 mm, it is *Vancouveria hexandra*, not illus.)

If leaves are large, three-parted; spikes of petalless flowers with white stamens rise above them, it is **Vanilla Leaf** →
Achlys triphylla

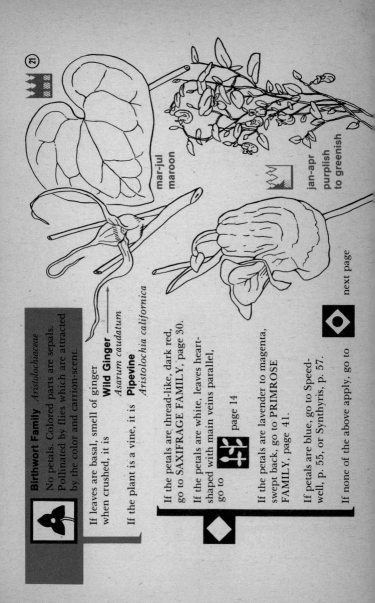

Birthwort Family *Aristolochiaceae*
No petals. Colored parts are sepals.
Pollinated by flies which are attracted
by the color and carrion-scent.

If leaves are basal, smell of ginger
when crushed, it is **Wild Ginger** ⟶
Asarum caudatum

If the plant is a vine, it is **Pipevine**
Aristolochia californica

mar–jul
maroon

jan–apr
purplish
to greenish

If the petals are thread-like, dark red,
go to SAXIFRAGE FAMILY, page 30.

If the petals are white, leaves heart-
shaped with main veins parallel,
go to 🌿 page 14

If the petals are lavender to magenta,
swept back, go to **PRIMROSE
FAMILY**, page 41.

If petals are blue, go to Speedwell, p. 55, or Synthyris, p. 57.

If none of the above apply, go to ◆ next page

may-jul
white

mar-jul
golden yellow

jan-sep
lemon yellow

② ◆ If flowers are tightly clustered, surrounded by four showy, petal-like bracts, it is **Bunchberry**
Cornus canadensis (Cornaceae)

If flowers have eight stamens, inferior ovary, go to EVENING PRIMROSE FAMILY, page 24.

If they have six stamens, superior ovary, it is

Mustard Family *Cruciferae*
Juice pungent. Flowers have four petals (narrowed at bases). Four sepals. Six stamens (four long and two short).

If flowers are bright yellow or orange, go to ⟶

If they're white, pale yellow or purple, go to next page

If leaves clasp the stem, and are often divided or compound, it is **Field Mustard**
Brassica campestris

If leaves are not clasping, are simple, it is **Wallflower**
Erysimum capitatum

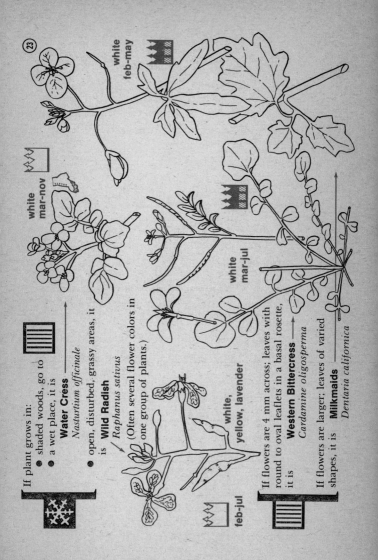

㉓

white
feb-may

white
mar-nov

(Often several flower colors in
one group of plants.)

white
mar-jul

If plant grows in:
● shaded woods, go to
● a wet place, it is
  Water Cress
  Nasturtium officinale
● open, disturbed, grassy areas, it
  is **Wild Radish**
  Raphanus sativus

white,
yellow, lavender

feb-jul

If flowers are 4 mm across; leaves with
round to oval leaflets in a basal rosette,
it is **Western Bittercress**
  Cardamine oligosperma

If flowers are larger; leaves of varied
shapes, it is **Milkmaids**
  Dentaria californica

Evening Primrose Family *Onagraceae.*
Simple leaves. Flower parts in fours.
Petals and sepals are attached above an
inferior ovary, which is often slender,
stem-like.

If flower is slender, tubular, with
scarlet sepals and petals; plant forming
mats, it is   **California Fuchsia** (illus. next page.)
      Zauschneria septentrionalis

If petals each are divided into three
lobes, bright pink, (may be striped or
streaked), it is   **Red Ribbons**
      Clarkia concinna

If petals are not lobed, and there are:

● four sepals, petals lilac-purple
  to rose (occasionally white)
  it is   **Fireweed**
        Epilobium angustifolium

  (A smaller plant, leaves
  opposite, is *Epilobium
  Watsonii.*)

● two sepals pushed to one side,
  petals pink, blotched with red,
  it is   **Farewell to Spring**
        Clarkia amoena

may-jul

jul-sep

jun-aug

If petals are partly or completely grown together at their edges, go to

If not, go to

If there is a mass of tightly packed, stemless small flowers which altogether look like one flower, go to SUNFLOWER FAMILY, page 42.

If not, go to   page 36

If flowers are in umbels, go to   page 33

If not, go to

If leaves are:

● compound, three-parted, it is   **Redwood Sorrel** →
Oxalis oregana
(Oxalidaceae)

mar-sep
white to lavender

● compound, pinnate, go to page 27.

● highly modified to trap insects, go to   next page

● simple, go to   next page

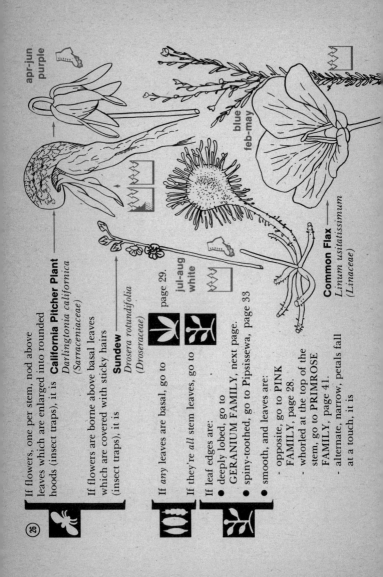

26

If flowers, one per stem, nod above leaves which are enlarged into rounded hoods (insect traps), it is **California Pitcher Plant** *Darlingtonia californica* (Sarraceniaceae)

apr-jun
purple

If flowers are borne above basal leaves which are covered with sticky hairs (insect traps), it is

Sundew — page 29.
Drosera rotundifolia (Droseraceae)

jul-aug
white

If *any* leaves are basal, go to

If they're *all* stem leaves, go to

If leaf edges are:

● deeply lobed, go to **PINK FAMILY**, page 28.

● spiny-toothed, go to **GERANIUM FAMILY**, next page.

● smooth, and leaves are:

  - opposite, go to Pipsissewa, page 33.

  - whorled at the top of the stem, go to **PRIMROSE FAMILY**, page 41.

  - alternate, narrow, petals fall at a touch, it is

Common Flax — *Linum usitatissimum* (Linaceae)

blue
feb-may

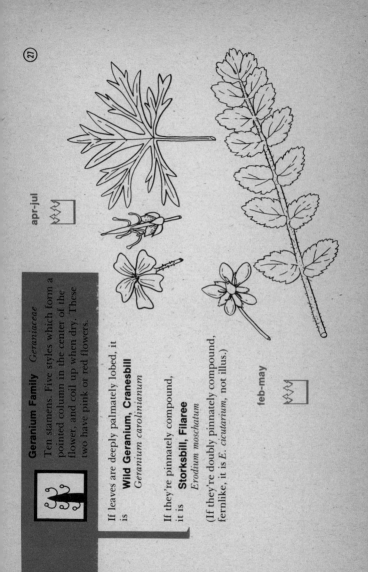

Geranium Family *Geraniaceae*

Ten stamens. Five styles which form a pointed column in the center of the flower, and coil up when dry. These two have pink or red flowers.

If leaves are deeply palmately lobed, it is **Wild Geranium, Cranesbill**
Geranium carolinianum

If they're pinnately compound, it is **Storksbill, Filaree**
Erodium moschatum

(If they're doubly pinnately compound, fernlike, it is *E. cicutarium*, not illus.)

apr–jul

feb–may

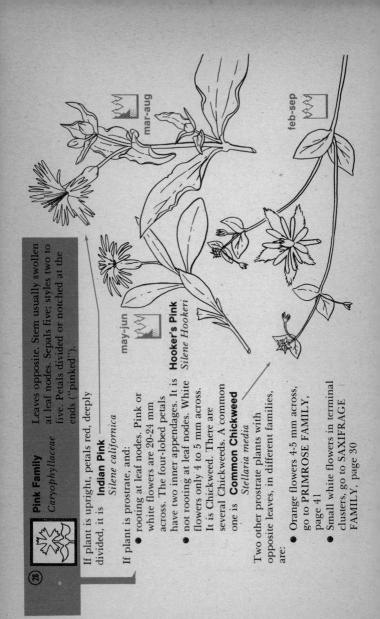

(28)

Pink Family
Caryophyllaceae

Leaves opposite. Stem usually swollen at leaf nodes. Sepals five; styles two to five. Petals divided or notched at the ends ("pinked").

If plant is upright, petals red, deeply divided, it is **Indian Pink**
Silene californica

If plant is prostrate, and:

● rooting at leaf nodes. Pink or white flowers are 20-24 mm across. The four-lobed petals have two inner appendages. It is **Hooker's Pink** *Silene Hookeri*

● not rooting at leaf nodes. White flowers only 4 to 5 mm across. It is Chickweed. There are several Chickweeds. A common one is **Common Chickweed**
Stellaria media

Two other prostrate plants with opposite leaves, in different families, are:

● Orange flowers 4-5 mm across, go to PRIMROSE FAMILY, page 41

● Small white flowers in terminal clusters, go to SAXIFRAGE FAMILY, page 30

may-jun

mar-aug

feb-sep

If leaf edges have lobes or teeth, go to SAXIFRAGE FAMILY, next page.

If leaf edges are smooth:
- ● leaves leathery, mottled white, go to Wild Wintergreen, page 33.
- ● leaves not leathery:

  - flowers hanging with petals turned back, go to PRIMROSE FAMILY, page 41.
  - flowers not so, it is

Portulaca or Purslane Family
Portulacaceae
Leaves fleshy but not thick. Stamens usually five, opposite petals. Two sepals.

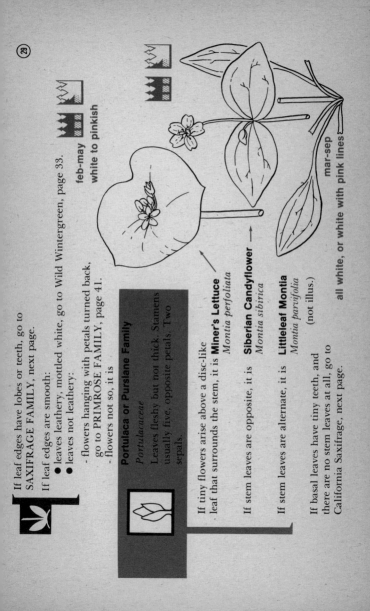

feb–may
white to pinkish

mar–sep
all white, or white with pink lines

If tiny flowers arise above a disc-like leaf that surrounds the stem, it is **Miner's Lettuce** *Montia perfoliata*

If stem leaves are opposite, it is **Siberian Candyflower** *Montia sibirica*

If stem leaves are alternate, it is **Littleleaf Montia** *Montia parvifolia* (not illus.)

If basal leaves have tiny teeth, and there are no stem leaves at all, go to California Saxifrage, next page.

Saxifrage Family *Saxifragaceae*

Stamens five or ten. Usually two hornlike styles. These plants are often found on stream banks or moist, rocky ledges.

If flower has *four* thread-like, dark red petals, it is **Piggyback Plant**
Tolmiea Menziesii

If petals are five, with:

● flowers in terminal clusters on a prostrate plant, leaves opposite, it is **Yerba de Selva**
Whipplea modesta

white
apr-jun

● flowers in a raceme, go to
● flowers in a panicle, go to next page

white
may-jun

If there are small basal leaves with teeth but not lobes, no stem leaves, it is **California Saxifrage**
Saxifraga californica

white
feb-jun

If there are many stem leaves and a tuft of basal leaves with three to five lobes, branching flower stalks, it is **Boykinia**
Boykinia elata

illus. next page

(30)

If petals are divided, go to [symbol] **next page**

If they're entire, and:

- curling out of an urn-shaped
calyx, (leaves shiny; leaf veins
and hairs on leaf stalks red) it is
Alum Root
Heuchera micrantha →

- not curling (sepals pink or white,
leaves dull, slightly fuzzy), it is
Sugar Scoops
Tiarella unifoliata ↗

may-jun
white

may-jul
white

white
jun-jul

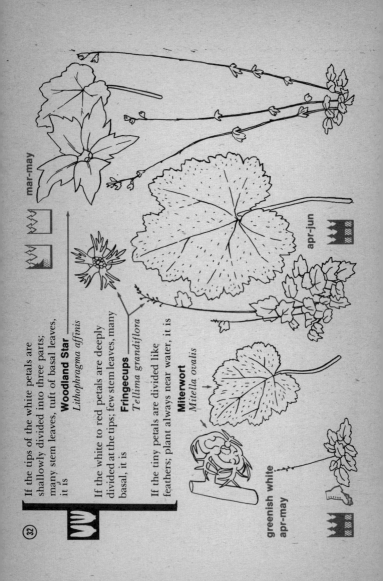

If the tips of the white petals are
shallowly divided into three parts;
many stem leaves, tuft of basal leaves,
it is
Woodland Star
Lithophragma affinis

If the white to red petals are deeply
divided at the tips; few stem leaves, many
basal, it is
Fringecups
Tellima grandiflora

If the tiny petals are divided like
feathers; plant always near water, it is
Miterwort
Mitella ovalis

mar-may

apr-jun

greenish white
apr-may

32

Wintergreen Family *Pyrolaceae*

Herbaceous perennials with tough, shiny leaves. Usually grow in deep forest leaf mold. Some members of this family have no chlorophyll.

If leaves appear basal (really stem leaves on an underground stem),
it is **Wild Wintergreen** —— *Pyrola asarifolia*

jun-aug
white

If leaves are in a whorl around the stem, with spiny-toothed margins;
it is **Pipsissewa, Prince's Pine**
Chimaphila umbellata

jun-aug
rose-purple

If plant is very big, with meter-long compound leaves, no parsley odor, fruit a berry, it is

Spikenard, Elk Clover
Aralia californica
(*Araliaceae*)

jun-aug
white to pink

If not so, go to PARSLEY FAMILY, next page.

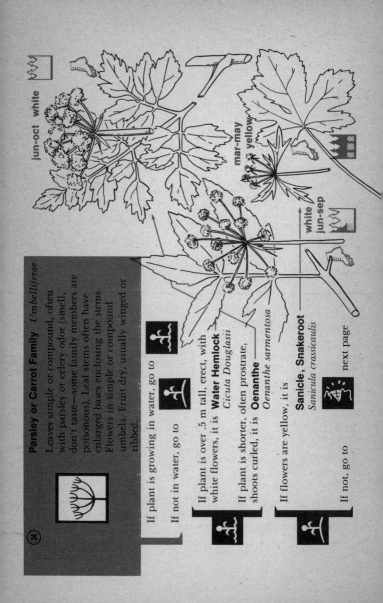

jun-oct white

mar-may yellow

white jun-sep

Parsley or Carrot Family *Umbelliferae*

Leaves simple or compound, often with parsley or celery odor (smell, don't taste—some family members are poisonous). Leaf stems often have enlarged bases enclosing the stems. Flowers in simple or compound umbels. Fruit dry, usually winged or ribbed.

If plant is growing in water, go to

If not in water, go to

If plant is over .5 m tall, erect, with white flowers, it is **Water Hemlock** *Cicuta Douglasii*

If plant is shorter, often prostrate, shoots curled, it is **Oenanthe** *Oenanthe sarmentosa*

If flowers are yellow, it is **Sanicle, Snakeroot** *Sanicula crassicaulis*

If not, go to   next page

(34)

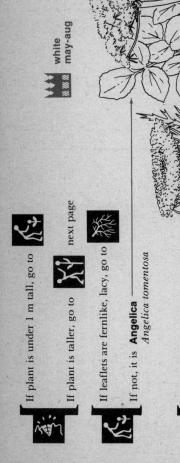

white
may-aug

white
may-sep

If plant is under 1 m tall, go to

If plant is taller, go to next page

If leaflets are fernlike, lacy, go to

If not, it is **Angelica**
Angelica tomentosa

If flowers are slightly enlarged at edges of flat umbels (which become cup-shaped with age) it is

Queen Anne's Lace, Wild Carrot
Daucus carota

If flowers at edges of umbels are same size; umbels not cup-shaped; stems purple-spotted, it is

Poison Hemlock (illus. next page)
Conium maculatum

apr-jul
white

apr-jul
white

mar-may
white

apr-sep

white to lavender

If leaflets are deeply divided, fernlike; stems purple-spotted, it is **Poison Hemlock**
Conium maculatum

If leaflets are large, undivided, and the stem seems swollen where the leaf stalks attach, it is **Cow Parsnip**
Heracleum lanatum

If plant is a vine, go to

If not, go to   next page

If petals are joined into an unlobed trumpet shape; leaves opposite each other and triangular, it is
Morning Glory, Bindweed
Convolvulus occidentalis
(Convolvulaceae)

If petals are lobed; leaves alternate, with tendrils, it is
Wild Cucumber, Manroot
Marah fabaceus
(Cucurbitaceae)

(Separate male and female flowers; ovary is spiny. If smooth, it is *M. oreganus*.

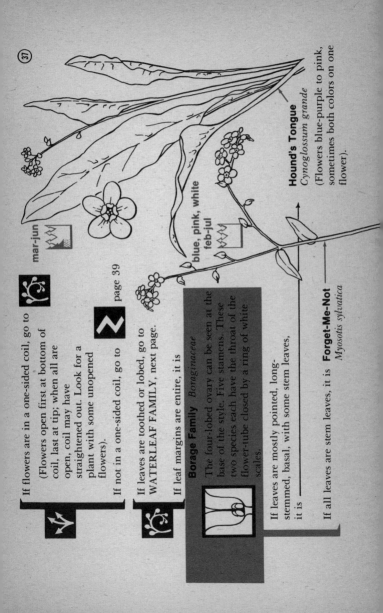

If flowers are in a one-sided coil, go to ⚘ **mar-jun**

(Flowers open first at bottom of coil, last at tip; when all are open, coil may have straightened out. Look for a plant with some unopened flowers).

If not in a one-sided coil, go to ⚡ page 39

If leaves are toothed or lobed, go to WATERLEAF FAMILY, next page.

If leaf margins are entire, it is ⚘

Borage Family *Boraginaceae*

The four-lobed ovary can be seen at the base of the style. Five stamens. These two species each have the throat of the flower-tube closed by a ring of white scales.

If leaves are mostly pointed, long-stemmed, basal, with some stem leaves, it is

If all leaves are stem leaves, it is **Forget-Me-Not**
Myosotis sylvatica

blue, pink, white feb-jul

Hound's Tongue
Cynoglossum grande

(Flowers blue-purple to pink, sometimes both colors on one flower).

Waterleaf Family *Hydrophyllaceae*

Flowers mostly in one-sided coils. Calyx deeply five-parted. Petals joined, five-lobed. Stamens five. Ovary superior.

If flower is whitish, and:

- leaves compound, pinnately divided into five lobes, it is
  Waterleaf
  Hydrophyllum tenuipes

- leaves simple, coarsely lobed, it is **Mist Maidens**
  Romanzoffia Suksdorfii

mar-may

apr-jun

may-jul

If flower is purple, leaves simple, lobed, hairy, it is ⟶

Bolander's Phacelia
Phacelia Bolanderi

38

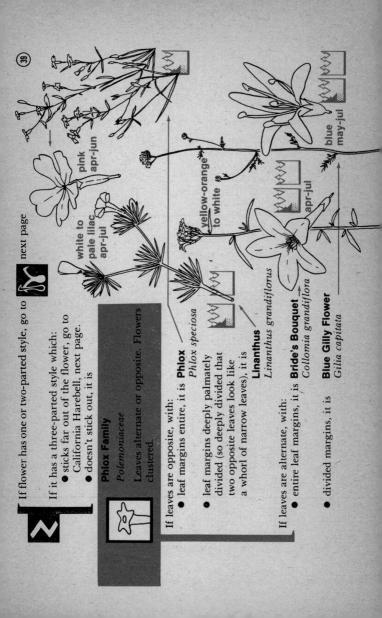

next page

If flower has one or two-parted style, go to next page

If it has a three-parted style which:

● sticks far out of the flower, go to California Harebell, next page.

● doesn't stick out, it is

Phlox Family
Polemoniaceae

Leaves alternate or opposite. Flowers clustered.

If leaves are opposite, with:

● leaf margins entire, it is **Phlox**
Phlox speciosa

pink
apr-jun

white to
pale lilac
apr-jul

● leaf margins deeply palmately divided (so deeply divided that two opposite leaves look like a whorl of narrow leaves), it is

Linanthus
Linanthus grandiflorus

yellow-orange
to white
apr-jul

If leaves are alternate, with:

● entire leaf margins, it is **Bride's Bouquet**
Collomia grandiflora

● divided margins, it is **Blue Gilly Flower**
Gilia capitata

blue
may-jul

40 If leaves are opposite, whorled or basal, go to ❋ next page

If they're alternate, it is

summer
white

Nightshade Family *Solanaceae*

Flowers five-lobed, folded like a fan in the bud. Five stamens, superior ovary, one stigma.

If plant is taller than .5 m, with coarse foliage, it is **Jimson Weed**
Datura stramonium

If plant is shorter, with slightly lobed leaves, it is **Nightshade**
Solanum nodiflorum

jun-sep
blue

California Harebell
Campanula prenanthoides
(*Campanulaceae*)

apr-nov
white to lavender

orange
mar-jul

white
apr-jul

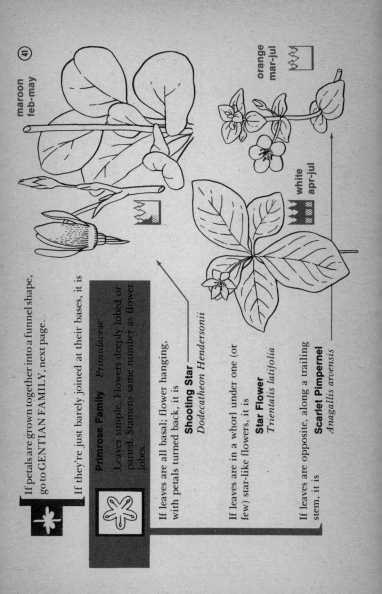

If petals are grown together into a funnel shape, go to GENTIAN FAMILY, next page.

If they're just barely joined at their bases, it is

Primrose Family *Primulaceae*

Leaves simple. Flowers deeply lobed or parted. Stamens same number as flower lobes.

If leaves are all basal; flower hanging, with petals turned back, it is

Shooting Star
Dodecatheon Hendersonii

If leaves are in a whorl under one (or few) star-like flowers, it is

Star Flower
Trientalis latifolia

If leaves are opposite, along a trailing stem, it is

Scarlet Pimpernel
Anagallis arvensis

may-aug   jun-aug

Gentian Family *Gentianaceae*

Plants have colorless, bitter juice.
Leaves usually simple, opposite.
Flowers stay on plant after withering.

If flowers are pink, it is **Pink Gentian**
Centaurium Davyi

If flowers are blue, it is **Blue Gentian, Oregon Gentian**
Gentiana oregana

Sunflower Family *Compositae*

A very large family, with flowers borne
on heads (see diagram). Pappus takes
the place of sepals. Each ovary bears
one seed.

If disk and ray flowers are both
present, go to
page 45

If ray flowers only, go to
next page

If disk flowers only, go to
next page

disk flower ⟶
ray flower
bracts
pappus
ovary

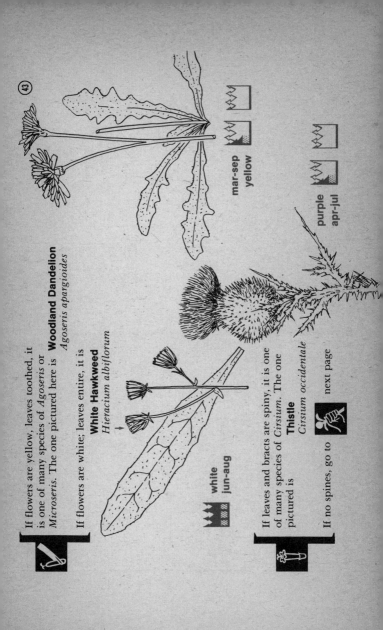

43

If flowers are yellow, leaves toothed, it is one of many species of *Agoseris* or *Microseris*. The one pictured here is **Woodland Dandelion**
Agoseris apargioides

If flowers are white; leaves entire, it is
White Hawkweed
Hieracium albiflorum

white
jun-aug

mar-sep
yellow

If leaves and bracts are spiny, it is one of many species of *Cirsium*. The one pictured is
Thistle
Cirsium occidentale

If no spines, go to   next page

purple
apr-jul

(44)

If leaves are:

- large, palmately lobed and
  veined, it is
  Western Coltsfoot
  Petasites palmatus
  (Flowers may precede leaves in
  early Spring.)

- triangular, not lobed, it is
  Trail Marker Plant
  Adenocaulon bicolor
  (Flowers tiny, greenish.)

- narrow, entire, it is
  Pearly Everlasting
  Anaphalis margaritacea
  (Yellow flowers are surrounded
  by papery, white, "everlasting"
  bracts.)

mar-apr
white, pink

jun-aug

jun-aug

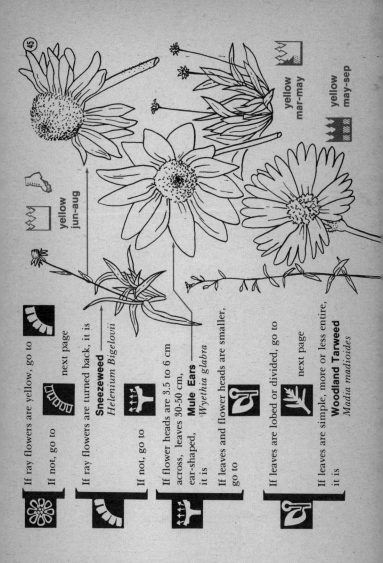

(45)

If ray flowers are yellow, go to

If not, go to   next page

If ray flowers are turned back, it is

Sneezeweed
Helenium Bigelovii

yellow
jun-aug

If not, go to

If flower heads are 3.5 to 6 cm
across, leaves 30-50 cm,
ear-shaped,   **Mule Ears**
it is   *Wyethia glabra*

If leaves and flower heads are smaller,
go to

yellow
mar-may

If leaves are lobed or divided, go to
next page

If leaves are simple, more or less entire,
it is   **Woodland Tarweed**
Madia madioides

yellow
may-sep

(46)

If pappus is hairy; and older leaves lack wool underneath it is **Groundsel**
Senecio Jacobaea

yellow
jul-aug

If pappus is scaly or absent; and older leaves are wooly, it is

Oregon Sunshine
Eriophyllum lanatum

yellow
apr-aug

next page

next page

If ray flowers are blue to purple, go to

next page

If ray flowers are white, and leaves are:

• finely divided, go to

• leaves *not* finely divided, and:

- in basal rosettes; flower heads under 3 cm across, with 30-80 rays, it is

English Daisy
Bellis perennis

white
apr-sep

- on stems; flower heads larger, with 15-30 rays, it is

Ox-Eye Daisy
Chrysanthemum leucanthemum

white
jun-aug

If tiny flower heads are in flat-topped
umbels, it is **Yarrow**
Achillea borealis, ssp. *californica*

white
mar-jun

If flower heads are not in umbels;
leaves foul-smelling, it is
Mayweed
Anthemis cotula

white
apr-aug

If your white-rayed flower doesn't
match the above, you may have a pale
specimen of the following:

If there are three rows of overlapping
bracts, it is **Coast Aster**
Aster chilensis

purple
jun-aug

If there are one or two rows of bracts,
which overlap only slightly, it is
Wild Daisy
Erigeron philadelphicus

pink
jun-aug

These two plants are over .4 m tall. If
rays are pink and the plant is much
smaller, see English Daisy, page 46.

If petals are completely free from each other, go to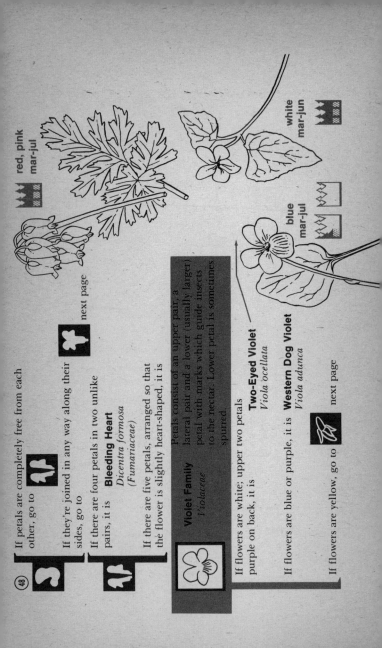

If they're joined in any way along their sides, go to → next page

If there are four petals in two unlike pairs, it is **Bleeding Heart**
Dicentra formosa
(Fumariaceae)

If there are five petals, arranged so that the flower is slightly heart-shaped, it is

Violet Family
Violaceae

Petals consist of an upper pair, a lateral pair and a lower (usually larger) petal with marks which guide insects to the nectar. Lower petal is sometimes spurred

If flowers are white; upper two petals purple on back, it is **Two-Eyed Violet**
Viola ocellata

If flowers are blue or purple, it is **Western Dog Violet**
Viola adunca

If flowers are yellow, go to → next page

red, pink
mar-jul

white
mar-jun

blue
mar-jun

If plants creep, root as they creep,
it is **Redwood Violet** ──
Viola sempervirens

If plants are upright, in clumps,
it is **Yellow Wood Violet** ──▸
Viola glabella

If the irregular flower seems to have all
petals free from each other, but is not a
Bleeding Heart or Violet, read the next
section.

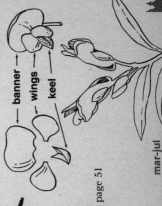

feb-apr
yellow

mar-jul
yellow

banner ──▸

wings ──▸

keel ──▸

Is the flower like this?

A large petal (banner) at the top,
two petals (wings) at the sides, and a
boat-shaped part (keel) at the bottom.
(The keel is formed of two joined
petals. Press on its tip to see the
stamens and pistil which it surrounds).

👉

🚫 page 51

If the flower is not like the above, go to

If it is, and leaves are:

● compound, go to PEA FAMILY,
  next page.
● simple, it is **Milkwort** ──▸
  Polygala californica
  (*Polygalaceae*)

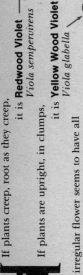

mar-jul
pink to lavender

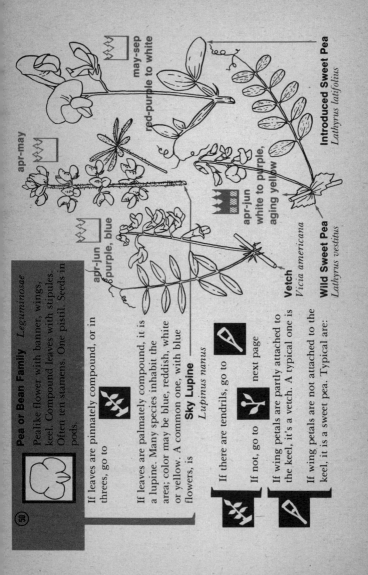

Pea or Bean Family *Leguminosae*

Pealike flower with banner, wings, keel. Compound leaves with stipules. Often ten stamens. One pistil. Seeds in pods.

If leaves are pinnately compound, or in threes, go to

If leaves are palmately compound, it is a lupine. Many species inhabit the area; color may be blue, reddish, white or yellow. A common one, with blue flowers, is —

Sky Lupine

Lupinus nanus

If there are tendrils, go to

If not, go to   next page

If wing petals are partly attached to the keel, it's a vetch. A typical one is

If wing petals are not attached to the keel, it is a sweet pea. Typical are:

apr-jun purple, blue

apr-may

may-sep red-purple to white

apr-jun white to purple, aging yellow

Vetch
Vicia americana

Wild Sweet Pea
Lathyrus vestitus

Introduced Sweet Pea
Lathyrus latifolius

⑤

apr-jun
white

apr-jun
yellow

yellow and rose
mar-jul

If plant is self-supporting, and:

- flowers are whitish; leaves aromatic, it is **California Tea** →
  Psoralea physodes

- flowers are yellow, in racemes; and there are large, leaf-like stipules, it is **False Lupine**
  Thermopsis macrophylla

If the plant is prostrate; flowers in umbels, it is **Bird's Foot Trefoil**
  Lotus formosissimus

If flower is reddish-brown tube, bent into a pipe shape, go to **BIRTHWORT FAMILY**, page 21.

If not as above, and the plant has *all* of these features:

- square stems,
- opposite or whorled leaves,
- aromatic leaves,

go to MINT FAMILY, next page

If the plant does not have *all* of the above features, go to

52

Mint Family *Labiatae*

Aromatic plants with mostly two-lipped flowers. Opposite or whorled leaves, square stems. Stamens four, two short and two long, attached to the flower tube. Single style with a four-parted ovary at the base which grows into four nutlets in fruit.

If flower is definitely two-lipped, go to

If flower is almost regular, not definitely two-lipped, go to   next page

If flowers are purple with lower lips which are:

- fringed; plant .1-.5 m tall, it is **Self Heal** *Prunella vulgaris*
- flat; plant .4-.8 m tall, it is **Wood Mint** *Stachys bullata*
- concave; plant .6-1 m tall, it is **Chamisso's Hedge Nettle** *Stachys Chamissonis*

If flowers are white; plant forms a long trailing vine, it is **Yerba Buena** *Satureja Douglasii*

apr-sep

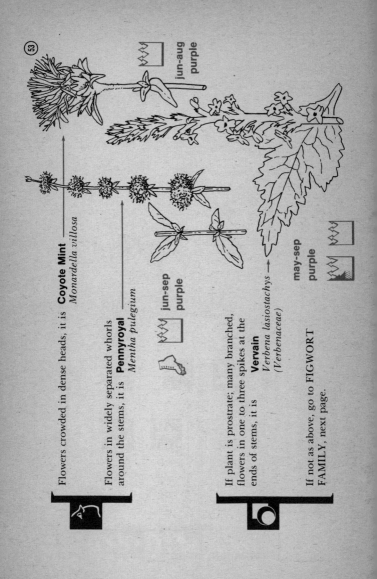

Flowers crowded in dense heads, it is **Coyote Mint**
Monardella villosa

jun-aug
purple

Flowers in widely separated whorls
around the stems, it is **Pennyroyal**
Mentha pulegium

jun-sep
purple

If plant is prostrate; many branched,
flowers in one to three spikes at the
ends of stems, it is
Vervain
Verbena lasiostachys →
(Verbenaceae)

may-sep
purple

If not as above, go to FIGWORT
FAMILY, next page.

Figwort or Snapdragon Family
Scrophulariaceae

Flowers often two-lipped. Stamens two, four or five. Pistil one or two-parted. Fruit a dry capsule with many seeds.

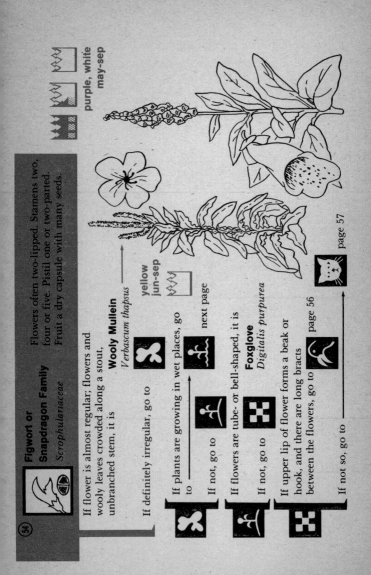

purple, white
may-sep

If flower is almost regular; flowers and wooly leaves crowded along a stout, unbranched stem, it is

Wooly Mullein
Verbascum thapsus

yellow
jun-sep

If definitely irregular, go to

If plants are growing in wet places, go to

next page

If not, go to

If flowers are tube- or bell-shaped, it is

Foxglove
Digitalis purpurea

If not, go to

page 56

If upper lip of flower forms a beak or hook, and there are long bracts between the flowers, go to

page 57

If not so, go to

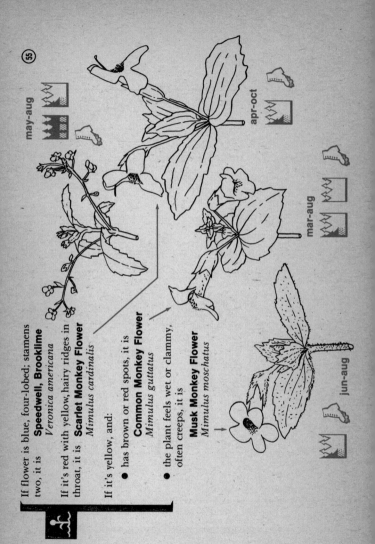

If flower is blue, four-lobed; stamens
two, it is **Speedwell, Brooklime**
Veronica americana

If it's red with yellow, hairy ridges in
throat, it is **Scarlet Monkey Flower**
Mimulus cardinalis

If it's yellow, and:

● has brown or red spots, it is
Common Monkey Flower
Mimulus guttatus

● the plant feels wet or clammy,
often creeps, it is

Musk Monkey Flower
Mimulus moschatus

may-aug

apr-oct

mar-aug

jun-aug

If bracts around or between flowers are green, leaflike, rather than brightly colored, it is **Parentucellia**
Parentucellia viscosa

If bracts around and between the flowers are colored, rather than green, and:

● flowers are red or orange, and:
- leaf is fernlike, it is **Indian Warrior**
Pedicularis densiflora

- leaf is simple, few-lobed, it is **Paintbrush** →
Castilleja affinis

● and flowers are white, purple or yellow, with little spots which make them resemble owl faces, it is

Owl's Clover →
Orthocarpus purpurascens

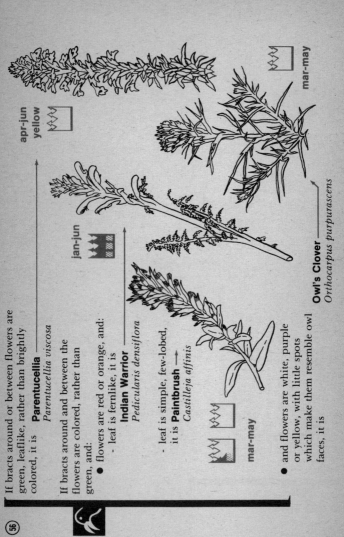

apr-jun
yellow

jan-jun

mar-may

mar-may

If flowers are red or red-brown, go to

If blue or purple, go to

If flowers are bright red, on a low plant, it is **Redwood Penstemon** →
Penstemon corymbosus

If red-brown, small flowers are on tall, upright stalks, it is

Figwort
Scrophularia californica

If reddish flowers are in regular whorls around the stem, see Chinese Houses.

If flowers form several whorls around the stem, upper petals of flowers usually a lighter shade than lower, it is

Chinese Houses
Collinsia heterophylla

If four-lobed flowers rise above kidney-shaped basal leaves, it is

Synthyris
Synthyris reniformis

jun-oct

feb-jun

mar-jun

feb-apr

By the year 2000, 2 out of 3 Americans could be illiterate.

It's true.

Today, 75 million adults… about one American in three, can't read adequately. And by the year 2000, U.S. News & World Report envisions an America with a literacy rate of only 30%.

Before that America comes to be, you can stop it… by joining the fight against illiteracy today.

Call the Coalition for Literacy at toll-free **1-800-228-8813** and volunteer.

Volunteer Against Illiteracy. The only degree you need is a degree of caring.

Ad Council   Coalition for Literacy